DATE DUE		

A MIDSUMMER NIGHT'S DREAM

THE GREENHAVEN PRESS
Literary Companion
TO BRITISH LITERATURE

A MIDSUMMER NIGHT'S DREAM

Stephen P. Thompson, *Book Editor*

David L. Bender, *Publisher*
Bruno Leone, *Executive Editor*
Bonnie Szumski, *Series Editor*

Greenhaven Press, Inc., San Diego, CA

Every effort has been made to trace the owners of copyrighted material. The articles in this volume may have been edited for content, length, and/or reading level. The titles have been changed to enhance the editorial purpose. Those interested in locating the original source will find the complete citation on the first page of each article.

Library of Congress Cataloging-in-Publication Data

Readings on A midsummer night's dream /
  Stephen P. Thompson, book editor.
      p. cm. — (The Greenhaven Press literary
  companion to British literature)
      Includes bibliographical references and index.
      ISBN 1-56510-691-1 (lib. : acid-free paper) —
  ISBN 1-56510-690-3 (pbk. : acid-free paper)
      1. Shakespeare, William, 1564–1616. Midsummer
  night's dream. 2. Comedy. I. Title: Midsummer night's
  dream. II. Thompson, Stephen P., 1953–   III. Series.

PR2827 .R43 2001
822.3'3—dc21

                                              00-025736

Cover photo: Giraudon/Art Resource
Library of Congress, 20

Copyright © 2001 by Greenhaven Press, Inc.
PO Box 289009
San Diego, CA 92198-9009
Printed in the U.S.A.

*"I have had a most rare vision.
I have had a dream, past the
wit of man to say what dream
it was. Man is but an ass if he
go about to expound this
dream. . . ."*

—Bottom, 4.1.203-6

Contents

Chapter 2: The Plot of *A Midsummer Night's Dream*

FOREWORD

*"'Tis the good reader that
makes the good book."*

Ralph Waldo Emerson

The story's bare facts are simple: The captain, an old and scarred seafarer, walks with a peg leg made of whale ivory. He relentlessly drives his crew to hunt the world's oceans for the great white whale that crippled him. After a long search, the ship encounters the whale and a fierce battle ensues. Finally the captain drives his harpoon into the whale, but the harpoon line catches the captain about the neck and drags him to his death.

A simple story, a straightforward plot—yet, since the 1851 publication of Herman Melville's *Moby-Dick*, readers and critics have found many meanings in the struggle between Captain Ahab and the whale. To some, the novel is a cautionary tale that depicts how Ahab's obsession with revenge leads to his insanity and death. Others believe that the whale represents the unknowable secrets of the universe and that Ahab is a tragic hero who dares to challenge fate by attempting to discover this knowledge. Perhaps Melville intended Ahab as a criticism of Americans' tendency to become involved in well-intentioned but irrational causes. Or did Melville model Ahab after himself, letting his fictional character express his anger at what he perceived as a cruel and distant god?

Although literary critics disagree over the meaning of *Moby-Dick*, readers do not need to choose one particular interpretation in order to gain an understanding of Melville's

9

novel. Instead, by examining various analyses, they can gain numerous insights into the issues that lie under the surface of the basic plot. Studying the writings of literary critics can also aid readers in making their own assessments of *Moby-Dick* and other literary works and in developing analytical thinking skills.

The Greenhaven Literary Companion Series was created with these goals in mind. Designed for young adults, this unique anthology series provides an engaging and comprehensive introduction to literary analysis and criticism. The essays included in the Literary Companion Series are chosen for their accessibility to a young adult audience and are expertly edited in consideration of both the reading and comprehension levels of this audience. In addition, each essay is introduced by a concise summation that presents the contributing writer's main themes and insights. Every anthology in the Literary Companion Series contains a varied selection of critical essays that cover a wide time span and express diverse views. Wherever possible, primary sources are represented through excerpts from authors' notebooks, letters, and journals and through contemporary criticism.

Each title in the Literary Companion Series pays careful consideration to the historical context of the particular author or literary work. In-depth biographies and detailed chronologies reveal important aspects of authors' lives and emphasize the historical events and social milieu that influenced their writings. To facilitate further research, every anthology includes primary and secondary source bibliographies of articles and/or books selected for their suitability for young adults. These engaging features make the Greenhaven Literary Companion series ideal for introducing students to literary analysis in the classroom or as a library resource for young adults researching the world's great authors and literature.

Exceptional in its focus on young adults, the Greenhaven Literary Companion Series strives to present literary criticism in a compelling and accessible format. Every title in the series is intended to spark readers' interest in leading American and world authors, to help them broaden their understanding of literature, and to encourage them to formulate their own analyses of the literary works that they read. It is the editors' hope that young adult readers will find these anthologies to be true companions in their study of literature.

INTRODUCTION

The plays of William Shakespeare have popular and timeless appeal. With the recent films *Shakespeare in Love*, starring Gwyneth Paltrow, and *A Midsummer Night's Dream*, starring Kevin Kline and Michelle Pfeiffer, diverse modern audiences have been newly charmed by the playwright and his works.

A Midsummer Night's Dream has long been one of Shakespeare's most popular and satisfying plays. It falls into the general category of light-hearted romantic comedy, and thus the outcome of the plot is predictable. In characterization, it is perhaps the weaver Nick Bottom who has the deepest revelation of the play, but finally he understands his vision to be only a dream. Further, he has not really changed or grown as a character; he is the same "bully Bottom" he was when the play began. Though plot and character are not its emphasis, the play remains a rich one in several respects. It is certainly a visual feast, loaded with elaborate costumes bedecking an Amazon queen and a slew of fairies, including their king and queen. It also supplies a number of memorable, profound images of fairy-tale quality, from a fairy applying love potion to a sleeping lover's eyes, to the Queen of Fairies asleep with a workman with an ass's head, a literal version of "beauty and the beast." The play also is rich with respect to its exploration of ideas and themes.

As one of Shakespeare's most frequently performed plays, *A Midsummer Night's Dream* has always seemed to offer something for everyone. Young lovers can see their confusions and infatuations depicted, ridiculed, and yet tolerantly acknowledged. More mature lovers can see the dignity and companionate friendship of Duke Theseus and his bride-to-be, Hippolyta, as well as the irrational jealousy and quarrelsome nature of the longtime couple Titania and Oberon. Those who hold love to be primarily an arbitrary and irrational matter of desire can find their view reinforced. Those who find love to be grounded primarily in mutual tolerance and rational understanding can find their view as well. Those who believe our fate is under the control of unseen powers or magical forces find this view in the play, as do those who believe we control our destinies if we can subject desire, passion, and imagination to the control of reason. Thus, the play is open to interpretation. Meanwhile, it makes us laugh. But this is not laughter *at* the confused characters; this is a more compassionate kind of laughter, a laughter of recognition of the kinds of ridiculous situations in which we find ourselves when under the influence of love, infatuation, and jealousy. When we are under the spell of love, even the Queen of Fairies can fall in love with an ass, and Shakespeare gleefully milks this ridiculous and ironic juxtaposition for all it's worth.

The essays collected in this Greenhaven Literary Companion are selected with the first-time reader of the play in mind. These essays, written by scholars at universities and colleges in the United States and England have been selected primarily for their ability to illuminate a particular facet of *A Midsummer Night's Dream.*

Whether read individually or together, the essays in this collection can provide a useful introduction to the issues and problems that frequently confront first-time readers of the play. These readings may also be useful in stimulating group discussion and in focusing written analysis.

WILLIAM SHAKESPEARE: A BIOGRAPHY

Though we know much less about the life of William Shakespeare than we would like to know, we know more about him than about any other English dramatist of the time, with the possible exception of Ben Jonson. We even know something of his brother Edmund, himself a would-be actor, and we have knowledge of another brother, Gilbert, who also ventured to London and opened a successful haberdashery, or men's clothing shop, in the St. Brides area of London. William was born on or very near April 23, 1564, in Stratford-upon-Avon, where his parents, John and Mary Shakespeare, were middle-class residents. The family home, William's birthplace, is still standing on Henley Street in Stratford. John was a glover, or glove maker, by trade, though he dabbled in a range of other business dealings, some more successfully than others. He achieved prominence in Stratford in middle age, first as a town alderman, or councilman, and then as bailiff, or mayor of Stratford. William was the first of John and Mary's eight children, only five of whom lived into adulthood. John's fortunes declined in the 1580s, but his successful son was determined to earn a coat-of-arms, a mark of prestige one could acquire for a price, for his father and the Shakespeare name, and this he accomplished in 1599.

SHAKESPEARE'S EDUCATION

At the King's New School in Stratford, William and his brothers received a strong education in typical Renaissance fashion: about nine hours of classroom time a day, six days a week, all year round. The heart of the curriculum was the Latin language and literature, and involved many hours of repetition in grammar and vocabulary, along with hours and hours spent translating texts from Latin and texts into Latin. In fact, in the upper forms, the boys were required to speak only Latin, and were censured for speaking English in the classroom. William had three successive teachers at the New School; each held a master's degree from Cambridge University and each was well paid by Elizabethan standards. As several scholars have noted, what William learned of classical literature at New School would be the near equivalent today to a college degree in Latin. There are suggestions in Shakespeare's plays that such a system could be a dreary and unsatisfying way to go through boyhood. In *As You Like It*, for example, the pessimist Jacques draws a verbal picture of

> the whining school-boy, with his satchel
> And shining morning face, creeping like snail
> Unwillingly to school.   (2.7. 144–46)

Though Shakespeare may have found school tedious at times, it is clear from his plays and poems that his schooling gave him a wide acquaintance with classical history and literature, which served him well in his dramatic career. His indebtedness to classical writers is everywhere in his plays, and a number of plays owe a strong debt to particular authors. The early *A Comedy of Errors* borrows heavily from the Roman playwright Plautus, for example, and *Titus Andronicus* owes much to the revenge tragedies of the Roman playwright Seneca. *Julius Caesar* and the later *Anthony and Cleopatra* are both derived and elaborated from the book *Parallel Lives* by the Greek historian and philosopher Plutarch. *A Midsummer Night's Dream* highlights Shakespeare's deep and abiding passion for the Roman poet Ovid.

MARRIAGE AND FAMILY

In November 1582, at age eighteen, William married Anne Hathaway, age twenty-six, the daughter of a prosperous neighboring farmer. Their first child, named Susanna, was born the following May. Twins, named Judith and Hamnet after Stratford friends and neighbors Judith and Hamnet Saddler, were born in February 1585, but Hamnet died in 1596 at the age of eleven. William lived in London each year during the theater season; why his family did not move to London with him we do not know. The public playhouses in London were closed during the summer months each year (due to the increased risk of the plague in hot weather), and Shakespeare presumably spent part or all of this time in Stratford, as his business dealings there would indicate.

We have no record at all of what Shakespeare did between 1585 and 1592, the so-called lost years. He may have helped in his father's business; he may have taught school, at least as a teaching assistant, for some of that time. He was almost certainly involved in the London theater by 1590, though, for by 1592 we know that several of his plays had been produced on the London stage, and he had achieved a measure of renown for these early efforts.

MAN OF THE LONDON THEATER

By 1592, Shakespeare was attracting serious public notice as a playwright in London, with three separate printed references to his three *Henry VI* plays. Scholars have ascertained that several other early plays, such as *Titus Andronicus* and *The Comedy of Errors*, had also been produced by this year. During these early years in London, Shakespeare published his only attempts at highbrow literature, the long narrative poems *Venus and Adonis* (1593) and *The Rape of Lucrece* (1594). In the fashion of the day, both poems were dedicated to a powerful patron, the earl of Southampton, and both poems were published by his fellow migrant from Stratford, the printer Richard Field. Shakespeare's accomplishments by 1594 were already so notable that he was invited to become a member (and resident playwright) of the just formed Lord Chamberlain's Men, which by virtue of its powerful patron, its accomplished actors, and its highly proficient playwright became the premier acting company of its day. The roster of the Lord Chamberlain's Men included such well-known actors as Richard Burbage, known for his skill in tragic roles, and Will Kempe, famous as the greatest comedian, comic actor, and comic dancer of his day. Other actors and members of the company included William Sly, Henry Condell, and John Heminges, the latter two of which collected and published the first edition of Shakespeare's collected plays in 1623, seven years after Shakespeare's death. As a shareholder in this very busy company, Shakespeare's early profits must have been substantial.

By 1597, Shakespeare's financial success enabled him to buy his family the second-largest house in Stratford, called New Place, a property with two barns, two large gardens, and ten fireplaces. Clearly he was doing well in his London career. Scholars conservatively estimate his earnings at about 200 pounds a year. By comparison, the well-paid, university-educated schoolmaster at Stratford had a salary of 20 pounds a year during this same period; many professional writers prior to Shakespeare were happy to earn 10 pounds in a year. Soon after the purchase of New Place in 1597, Shakespeare put out feelers to buy more land around Stratford, but he ended up postponing further purchases of land until 1602, when he bought 127 acres of land in and around Stratford for the considerable sum of 320 pounds. In 1605, he made his largest investment in Stratford, in an amount equivalent to several hundred thousand dollars in today's money, when he purchased a half-share of a tithe in the Stratford town corporation for the sum of 440 pounds. After his mother's death in 1608 (his father had died in 1601), Shakespeare also held title to the large house in which he was born on Henley Street, which today is called simply Shakespeare's Birthplace. He apparently retired to Stratford around 1611, where he died in 1616 at the age of fifty-two. There he is buried inside the Holy Trinity Church.

Most of Shakespeare's later income came from the one-eighth share he held in ownership of the Globe Theatre, which was opened to the public in July 1599. The Lord Chamberlain's Men had held the lease at the Theatre playhouse since their formation, but when the lease was due to expire, they had a conflict with their landlord. Instead of signing a new, disadvantageous lease, the company dismantled the actual Theatre building (which they legally owned) around Christmas 1598 and began to rebuild it on the south bank side of the Thames River. Shakespeare became one of eight major shareholders in the ownership of the new theater, which they renamed the Globe. Most of Shakespeare's plays composed between 1599 and 1608 opened at the Globe, including *Julius Caesar, Hamlet,* and the other great tragedies, and Shakespeare's company flourished. When Queen Elizabeth died in 1603, her successor, James I, decided to take over the patronage of Shakespeare's acting company himself, and the Lord Chamberlain's Men became at that point simply the King's Men. Reflecting their new name, the company performed more often at the royal court than ever before, providing 177 court performances between 1603 and 1613, in productions of many of Shakespeare's plays as well as plays by other writers.

SHAKESPEARE'S EARLY COMEDIES

Though we do not know when or why Shakespeare gravitated to London, we can deduce that his career as a playwright commenced sometime around 1590, probably with his series of four history plays about the Wars of the Roses:

Henry VI, Parts 1, 2, and 3, and *Richard III.* Most of Shakespeare's history plays were written in the first half of his career; most of his tragedies were composed in the second half. He wrote comedies throughout his career, although they tended to be lighter in tone in the early years and darker and more problematic in later years. *A Midsummer Night's Dream* is one of Shakespeare's early romantic comedies, written around 1595, part of a group of early comedies that includes *The Merchant of Venice, As You Like It,* and *Much Ado About Nothing.* Peter Hyland provides this useful overview of Shakespearean comedy:

> Typically a comedy begins with a moment of social disruption: a daughter will not obey her father, a man banishes a brother, a man or woman rejects a lover, a man falsely suspects the woman he loves. This disruption opens the way for a series of plot complications that might include inversions in which women are given the power of men, or servants the power of masters. That is, the normal social hierarchical structure is turned upside-down. This sense of comedy as carnival liberation is often intensified by having the characters move from the threatening world of court or city to the green and magical world of nature, as the lovers of *A Midsummer Night's Dream* flee to the woods outside Athens, or the characters of *As You Like It* go out to the forest of Arden. The comic experience often involves confusions of identity, a failure to distinguish appearance from reality that is underscored by confusions and slippages in language, the linguistic play of puns and malapropisms and the subversion of rhetorical and logical structure. The opening disruption is ultimately settled, often by magic or something that looks like magic, by a sudden revelation of identity or reversal of attitude, opening the way for a final harmonious resolution through marriage. Marriage implies natural harmony through fertility and the renewal of the cycle of life, and it also implies social harmony, being the fundamental pattern on which society is built.[1]

The patterns described by Hyland fit the action of most Shakespearean comedies, especially that of the earlier romantic comedies. Several of the later comedies, though, challenge the "harmonious resolution" noted by Hyland, for they contain such complications as awkward marriage proposals, forced marriages, characters that seem unworthy of forgiveness, or revelations that seem unbelievable.

A Midsummer Night's Dream suffers none of these complications in its resolution. In fact, the main action of the play is wrapped up at the end of act 4, and the final act consists of a wedding celebration and a play-within-a-play performance. It is a lighthearted romantic comedy that offers more satisfaction than unanswered questions.

THE BACKGROUND OF *A MIDSUMMER NIGHT'S DREAM*

A Midsummer Night's Dream is one of Shakespeare's few plays with an original plotline; most of Shakespeare's plots were borrowed from previously published historical or literary texts. Yet the play's characters and language can be traced to numerous literary sources. Shakespeare borrows details, names, aspects of characterization, and more from a wide range of sources in this play. Chaucer's *Knight's Tale* and *Merchant's Tale,* Plutarch's "Life of Theseus" in his *Parallel Lives,* Ovid's long poem *Metamorphoses,* and John Lyly's play *Gallathea* are just a few of the texts contributing something to the play. But this is a play in which the most profound influences are not derived from literary texts. The larger influences in *A Midsummer Night's Dream* come from village culture and country folklore, and from the traditions and observances of important country holidays.

Though *A Midsummer Night's Dream* is ostensibly set in Athens, Greece, perhaps no other Shakespeare play so fully evokes the English countryside and its inhabitants. The early morning hunting party of Duke Theseus, the familiar spirits of the woods such as Puck, the small-town bumpkins Bottom and his crew, and the detailed lists and descriptions of woodland plants and flowers—all these powerfully reflect the small-town milieu of Shakespeare's own upbringing. The play's depiction of the woodland fairies and Puck, or Robin Goodfellow, is derived primarily from English folklore, from the stories of mischief and misadventure that found true believers throughout the countryside. Nick Bottom and his crew of "mechanicals," or tradesmen who work with their hands, could be found in every village in England, for every village had need of a good weaver, a carpenter, a tinker, a tailor, and a joiner. But perhaps only someone who had lived among such workers could depict them in such detail, with their below-average intelligence and foibles, but also with their camaraderie, their cultural aspirations, and their basic decency.

More than any other Shakespeare play, *A Midsummer Night's Dream* reflects the form and spirit of an Elizabethan holiday. The play continually alludes to both the May Day celebration and the festival of Midsummer Eve, both of which were associated with revelry, sexual license, magic, and mistakes of all kinds. Holiday celebrations were an integral feature of Elizabethan society, for they provided release from the tedium and constriction of the workaday world. As scholar C.L. Barber describes it:

We can get hold of the spirit of Elizabethan holidays because they had form. "Merry England" was merry chiefly by virtue of its community observances of periodic sports and feast days. Mirth took form in morris-dances, sword-dances, wassailings, mock ceremonies of summer kings and queens and of lords of misrule, mummings, disguisings, masques–and a bewildering variety of sports, games, shows, and pageants improvised on traditional models. Such pastimes were a regular part of the celebration of marriage, of the village wassail or wake, of Candlemas, Shrove Tuesday, Hocktide, May Day, Whitsuntide, Midsummer Eve, Harvest-home, Halloween, and the twelve days of the Christmas season ending with Twelfth Night. Custom prescribed, more or less definitely, some ways of making merry at each occasion. The seasonal feasts were not, as now, rare curiosities to be observed by folklorists in remote villages, but landmarks framing the cycle of the year, observed with varying degrees of sophistication by most elements in the society. Shakespeare's casual references to the holidays always assume that his audience is entirely familiar with them.[2]

THE THEMES OF THE PLAY

Thematically, *A Midsummer Night's Dream* is primarily a play about romantic love and its progress to the state of marriage. Shakespeare gives us a running commentary on the frustrations, yearnings, and pitfalls of love in a variety of manifestations. "The course of true love never did run true" (1.1.136), as Lysander laments. The initial focus is on the tangled affairs of four young lovers, but a counterpoint to their dilemma is posed by two more mature sets of lovers. Three stages of love are thus explored: the deep infatuation and passionate young love of Hermia and Lysander and Helena and Demetrius; the balanced, almost rational love of Duke Theseus and Hippolyta; and the strong-willed, argumentative love of the long-married Oberon and Titania. While the first and third of these groups experience trials and tribulations, all four sets of lovers find harmony by play's end. But the power of love or infatuation to transform our perspective is visualized for us through the image of the sublime enchantment of Titania, Queen of Fairies, holding the ass-headed Bottom the weaver in her arms. Thematically, the sublime and the ridiculous meet in the condition of passionate love. Perhaps this is what Helena means earlier in the play when she says, "Love looks not with the eyes but with the mind" (1.1.234).

Artist Henry Fuseli depicts a scene from A Midsummer Night's Dream. *The Swiss-born Fuseli was a much respected painter during the Romantic period.*

But the romantic love explored in *A Midsummer Night's Dream* is linked to other prominent themes in the play. The play also raises persistent questions about the irrational side of romantic attraction and the role of imagination in love, presented initially through the infatuation of the young lovers. As the action develops, a kind of dialectic is established between the insistent demands of irrational love and desire and the more measured, mature love that claims a basis in reason and understanding. The play presents us with an ongoing dialogue about the relative merits of reason and imagination. British scholar R.A. Foakes offers the following overview of the debate, along with his assessment:

> Some critics have felt that the play affirms the importance of the world of dreams or fantasy, and shows that reason impoverishes the imagination; others have recognised the extent to which it also exposes the absurdities of the imagination and gives approval to the voice of reason. It seems to me that *A Midsummer Night's Dream* achieves a splendid balance between the two; if the imagination makes possible visions and experiences otherwise inaccessible, and liberates natural energies from the restraints of reason, those visions and experiences are only given form and meaning through the reason. Such a view fits in well with the thinking of Shakespeare's age about the relation of imagination to reason. . . . The return to

order in Act 5 fulfills the pattern of the play, which expresses the need for and exposes the limitations of both reason and imagination.[5]

Other scholars contend that in the end the playwright sides with the powers of imagination and love rather than with reason, for the whole play is presented as if it were the literal performance of a dream. They point to the fact that Duke Theseus, confident in the power of reason, has no clue about the fairies that the audience has seen at work, even at the end of the play. Oberon provides the blessings on the retiring pairs of lovers and Puck provides the play's epilogue, in effect giving fairyland the "last word" in the play. But readers and audiences must ultimately come to their own conclusions on this issue.

A Midsummer Night's Dream also reflects self-consciousness about the creative act itself. The farcical play-within-a-play of the mechanicals serves as a vehicle for continual commentary about the strengths and weaknesses of actors and their role in conveying a piece of dramatic fiction to an audience. There are also reflections about the role of the audience in bringing a play to life, reflections about what Keats called the suspension of disbelief of the audience and the necessity for the audience to supply imagination for the success of any play. Duke Theseus also reflects on the creative act, suggesting that the inspiration of the poet is akin to the passions of love and the state of madness:

> The lunatic, the lover and the poet
> Are of imagination all compact:
> The one sees more devils than vast hell can hold;
> That is the madman: the lover, all as frantic,
> Sees Helen's beauty in a brow of Egypt:
> The poet's eye, in a fine frenzy rolling,
> Doth glance from heaven to earth, from earth to heaven;
> And as imagination bodies forth
> The forms of things unknown, the poet's pen
> Turns them to shapes and gives to airy nothing
> A local habitation and a name.   (5.1. 1–22)

In a play that tries to convince its audience that it has only witnessed a dream, the shapes of the play may well come close to being "airy nothing." And yet, there is something of "great constancy" about it, as Hippolyta says of the young lovers' experience in the woods. Duke Theseus dismisses the "fantasies" of the lunatic, lover, and poet in favor of "cool reason," but of course his perspective is very limited. He has no idea what "really" happened to the lovers in woods. And of course, the lovers' perspective is equally limited. It is the fairies of the play who have the widest perspective on the action, and, when the prankish Puck addresses the audience directly at the end, we may wonder whether the fairy perspective also encompasses our own as audience. This leads us to consideration of the central role of magic and the supernatural in the play.

THE SUPERNATURAL ELEMENTS OF THE PLAY

If Duke Theseus and his tolerant, rational view of life is intended as the play's wisest commentary on the romantic misadventures the audience has witnessed, then why bring the fairies back into the play, into the court and out of their "natural" habitat in the woods? By giving fairyland the last word in the play, Shakespeare seems to contradict, or at least ironically undercut, the belief of the human characters that they have reentered a world of order and rationality after their ordeal in the forest. What then are we to make of the power of these fairies? British scholar Helen Hackett provides this commentary on the fairies and what their power represents:

> The fairies in the play are in some ways rather like the gods in ancient Greek or Roman mythology, in that they possess super-human powers and yet are subject to human emotions like jealousy, rage, and revenge; and when they act on these emotions, any mortals who happen to cross their paths can find themselves helplessly embroiled in the consequences. Like the pagan gods, the fairies occupy a different plane of action from that of the mortals, yet at the same time have the ability to intervene in the affairs of humans, affecting them in ways which are baffling and mystifying. This often makes the fairies seem like personifications of the kinds of mysterious and ungovernable external forces—such as fate, or luck, or nature, or love—which can override the attempts of humans to plan and control our own destinies. Such forces are unsusceptible to rational control, and the sense that they are unleashed and allowed free play in this drama is enhanced by its setting in a dream-world where anything seems possible.[4]

The central role of the fairies in arranging the love affairs of the humans in the play suggests that the fairies may represent above all else the power or force in nature that compels human beings to mate; they represent a force of nature that cannot be resisted or denied. Thus Oberon's appropriate role at play's end is to provide a blessing of fertility over the marriage beds of the three pairs of human lovers.

The existence of the fairyland within the play *A Midsummer Night's Dream* lends a deep undercurrent of mystery to the play and our experience of it. If the characters of the play must woo and mate "under the influence" of the fairies, then we also must wonder how much of romance and affection are ultimately under our control in our own realm. It is the special genius of *A Midsummer Night's Dream* to provide audiences the vicarious experience of the confusion, wonder, and mystery that all lovers eventually feel in the "dream" of romantic love.

NOTES

1. Peter Hyland, *An Introduction to Shakespeare: The Dramatist in his Context.* New York: St. Martin's, 1996, p. 137.
2. C.L. Barber, *Shakespeare's Festive Comedy: A Study of Dramatic Form and Its Relation to Social Custom.* Princeton, NJ: Princeton University Press, 1959, pp. 5–6.
3. R.A. Foakes, Introduction to *A Midsummer Night's Dream.* Cambridge: Cambridge University Press, 1984, pp. 37–38.
4. Helen Hackett, *A Midsummer Night's Dream.* Plymouth, UK: Northcote House, 1997, pp. 2–3.

CHARACTERS AND PLOT

CHARACTER SUMMARIES

Nick Bottom: A weaver by trade and an enthusiastic ham of an actor; Bottom provides the spark and energy behind the mechanicals' desire to put on a play for Duke Theseus's wedding celebration. While rehearsing in the woods, Bottom is given the head of an ass by Puck. His noises awaken the enchanted queen of the fairies, Titania, who falls in love with him. After awakening the next morning, the restored Bottom has no words to describe his "vision." He returns to Athens to enthusiastically perform the play.

Demetrius: Suitor for the hand of Hermia; Demetrius has won the endorsement of Hermia's father, Egeus, but not the love of Hermia. Previously, Demetrius had wooed and become "betrothed" to Hermia's friend Helena. In the woods, Puck enchants him into loving Helena. When they all awake from their night in the woods, he discovers that he really does love Helena and not Hermia.

Egeus: The hard-hearted father of Hermia; he insists on forcing his daughter to marry the young man of his choice, Demetrius. After the young lovers return from the woods, he is overruled by Theseus, who allows Hermia to marry Lysander.

Helena: Hermia's best friend; she loves Demetrius, who has switched his affections to Hermia. She tells Demetrius of the flight of Hermia and Lysander, hoping to win back his love. Lost in the woods, she becomes the object of affection of both Lysander and Demetrius, who are under the spell of Puck. She believes she is the target of a practical joke; but when morning comes, she is reunited with Demetrius, who now loves her.

Hermia: Daughter of Egeus; she loves Lysander and refuses to marry her father's choice, Demetrius, who claims to love her too. She elopes with Lysander, but becomes sepa-

rated from him in the woods at night. When the fairy Puck
goes to work, she is rejected by both of her suitors, who turn
their attentions to her best friend, Helena. She awakes from
her night in the woods to the renewed love of Lysander,
whom she marries.

Hippolyta: Queen of the Amazons and bride-to-be of Duke
Theseus; like Theseus, she anticipates the celebration of her
imminent wedding. When the four young lovers return from
the woods, Hippolyta expresses more empathy than Theseus
does for the fantastic nature of their experience. She acknowledges the truth found in imagination while Theseus
endorses human reason.

Lysander: Hermia's true love; after their match is rejected
by Egeus, Lysander convinces Hermia to elope with him. He
is an impulsive but true-hearted lover, at least until Puck
anoints his eyes with a potion that makes him reject Hermia
and fall in love with Helena. On awakening from his midsummer night's dream, he is reunited with Hermia.

Oberon: Though he is king of the fairies, Oberon behaves
in a very human way. He argues with his queen, Titania,
over an orphan boy Titania has been raising. In his anger,
Oberon puts a spiteful spell on a sleeping Titania, so that
when she awakens, she falls in love with Bottom. Oberon is
also sympathetic to the plight of the four lost lovers in the
woods, and he plots to match them appropriately. When he
sees the predicament of Titania, Oberon regrets his spiteful
act, and he and Titania are reconciled.

Philostrate: Master of the revels for Duke Theseus; it is his
job to screen the potential entertainments for the duke's
wedding. He rejects the mechanicals as a possibility, but he
is overruled by Theseus.

Puck: Also called Robin Goodfellow, Puck is a servant of
Oberon, king of the fairies. Well known as a mischief maker,
he takes on, at the direction of Oberon, duties similar to
those of the matchmaker Cupid. When he mistakenly
matches the wrong young men and women, Oberon directs
him to set things right. Puck is gleeful about the perplexities
of humans in love, but he also blesses the marriage beds of
the three couples. Puck delivers the play's Epilogue directly
to the audience.

Peter Quince: A carpenter and the stage manager of the
craftsmen's play *Pyramus and Thisbe,* Quince must wrestle
with Bottom's desire to play all the play's parts and with the

anxieties of the mechanicals that they might frighten their audience. Quince and the other mechanicals flee rehearsal when Puck puts an ass's head on Bottom. When Bottom returns to Athens as himself, they happily stage their play, with Quince as speaker of the Prologue.

Snug, Flute, Snout, Starveling: Along with Bottom and Peter Quince, these are the members of the mechanicals' troupe of actors. They will perform a most ridiculous version of the comic tragedy *Pyramus and Thisbe* at the duke's wedding act 5.

Theseus: The duke of Athens, who has recently conquered the queen of the Amazons, Hippolyta in battle and then won her love; their wedding is the event toward which the action of the play builds. Theseus is generally good-natured and tolerant, but he is also patriarchal and overly rational. He initially backs Egeus in his demand that Egeus's daughter Hermia marry Demetrius, whom she does not love. But later in the play he overrules Egeus and allows the young lovers their own choice of partners.

Titania: The queen of the fairies, Titania is adamant about keeping control of her orphan boy. She fights Oberon on this because of her close companionship with the boy's mother, who has died. The victim of Oberon's tricks, Titania falls in love with Bottom, who wears the head of an ass. When she awakes, she graciously accepts a reconciliation with Oberon.

PLOT SUMMARY

The plot of *A Midsummer Night's Dream* is structured around four interacting groups of characters: the court group of Theseus, duke of Athens; a set of four "perplexed" young lovers; the quarreling king and queen of the fairies and their entourage; and a group of local craftsmen, or "mechanicals." By means of accident and fairy mischief, these four sets of characters interact in extraordinary ways, highlighted by the brief love affair between Titania, queen of the fairies, and Bottom, leader of the mechanicals. The plot has three main phases, moving from the rational world of law and order in Theseus's court, into a world of fantasy and confusion in the nighttime woods, and then back into the court world of order, harmony, and marriage.

As the play opens, Duke Theseus and his bride-to-be, Hippolyta are calmly discussing their upcoming wedding in four days. Hippolyta, legendary queen of the Amazons, has recently been conquered in battle by Theseus and his troops, but now he has won her love. Their discussion is interrupted by the urgent suit of Egeus, Hermia's father, who petitions Theseus to force Hermia to marry the suitor he has chosen. Hermia loves Lysander, but her father insists that she marry his choice, Demetrius. Demetrius claims to love Hermia, though he has previously wooed Hermia's best friend, Helena, who still loves him. Duke Theseus hears the case and decides that Hermia must follow her father's wishes as dictated by Athenian law, which states that fathers have the right to pick their daughter's mate. Hermia and Lysander then plan to flee Athens that night through the woods to the remote house of Lysander's aunt, where they can be secretly married. When they leave, they are followed by Demetrius and Helena.

Meanwhile, a group of local craftsmen, led by Nick Bottom the weaver, has decided to put on a play for the wedding celebration of Theseus and Hippolyta. The play they choose is the tragic love story of Pyramus and Thisbe. The craftsmen are enthusiastic yet concerned lest they scare the ladies of the court with their representations of violence. They decide to repair to the forest that night to rehearse their play in private. In that very forest, the king and queen of fairies, Oberon and Titania, have been quarreling over the possession of an orphan boy. In his anger Oberon turns to dirty tricks to humiliate Titania; he will apply a magic love potion to her eyes while she sleeps so that she will love the first thing she sees upon awakening. He does this when he finds her sleeping.

Moreover, Oberon witnesses the confusion of the four young lovers as they become lost in the woods, and he instructs his mischievous fairy Puck to set things right by putting the same love juice on the eyes of Demetrius so he will love Helena. Puck comes across the play rehearsal of the craftsmen and decides to give Bottom the weaver the head of an ass, which frightens away his companions. When Bottom begins to sing, Titania awakes, sees him, and instantly falls in love with him. Meanwhile, Puck has accidentally put the love potion onto the eyes of Lysander, who awakens to see Helena and not his true love, Hermia. In trying to correct his error, Puck applies the juice to Demetrius, who also spies Helena when he wakes. The confusion of the lovers in the woods is now at its peak, epitomized by the infatuation of the queen of fairies with a weaver with an ass's head.

When the four young lovers fall asleep from exhaustion, Puck is finally able to match the lovers in the proper pairs. Oberon then regrets his trick on Titania, so he releases her from her spell and they are reconciled. Duke Theseus and Hippolyta have risen early to go hunting, when they happen across the sleeping young lovers. Since all four seem to know their hearts when they awaken, Theseus overrules Egeus and proclaims that the young lovers will be married at his own nuptial. Bottom awakens, too, from his "most rare vision," and rejoins his comrades in time to present their play.

In trying to understand the fantastic story told by the young lovers about their experience in the woods, Theseus and Hippolyta debate the relative powers of reason and imagination. As part of their wedding celebration, Theseus selects the ostensible tragedy of Pyramus and Thisbe, to be performed by Bottom and his troupe of mechanicals. Through the incompetence of the craftsmen, the play becomes a hilarious travesty, but Theseus cautions against judging such efforts too harshly. As the three sets of lovers go to bed, Puck and Oberon appear to bless their marriage beds with peace, health, and fertility.

CHAPTER 1

Social and Cultural Contexts of *A Midsummer Night's Dream*

READINGS ON
A MIDSUMMER NIGHT'S DREAM

The Play's Festive Spirit

Gail Kern Paster and Skiles Howard

In the following essay, Shakespeare scholars Gail
Kern Paster and Skiles Howard trace the cultural
practices of the holiday season encompassing May
Day and Midsummer Eve, and they suggest ways in
which Shakespeare evokes the festive spirit of these
holidays to enrich and animate his play. They also
examine contemporary critiques and defenses of
these festive celebrations, revealing their association
with license, rebellion, and potential violence. Paster
is currently editor of *Shakespeare Quarterly* and professor of English at George Washington University;
Howard teaches at Rutgers University.

Intoxicated by the holiday ambiance of *A Midsummer Night's
Dream*, and enthralled by the preposterous yet all-too-familiar
amorous plights of the play's lovers, readers and playgoers
may not be aware of the intricate relationship between
forms of celebration and the social changes taking place in
early modern England, or of the intense controversy sur-
rounding holiday customs. The action of *A Midsummer
Night's Dream* is propelled by two celebrations, the popular
holiday of Midsummer's Eve, and the elite ceremony of a
royal marriage. Each was a significant and resonant occasion for Shakespeare's audience, and the sights, sounds, sentiments, and fantasies associated with these popular and
court celebrations are crucial to the play. But these occasions have long vanished from our cultural memory and today most of us have no knowledge of how they looked or
what they signified.

As the play begins, Duke Theseus and Hippolyta antici-
pate a court wedding of pomp, triumph, and reveling
(1.1.19), and the young lovers Hermia and Lysander flee into
the woods where the popular holiday of May Day is observed
(1.1.165–67), evoking the contrast between elite and popular

festivity that by the 1590s had become progressively marked. The increasing distinction between popular and elite festivity in early modern England confirmed and strengthened the corresponding hierarchies of ruler and ruled, gentlemen and common people, and men and women, social hierarchies that expedited the formation of the modern family and nation. . . .

We might imagine the Maygame as an all-embracing bucolic idyll, part of a shared rural heritage universally enjoyed by all ranks and conditions in a "merry England"; but this communal Maygame, if it ever existed, had certainly vanished by Shakespeare's time. Instead, there were many "Maydays" in the collective imagination, contradictory and associated with specific social interests, which ranged from John Stow's vision of a unifying celebration in *A Survey of London* (1603) to Philip Stubbes's nightmare of destructive license in *The Anatomy of Abuses* (1583). In traditional critical readings of the play, the ending of *A Midsummer Night's Dream* stages the absorption of a human world of conflict into the cyclical eternity of a great creating nature that is part fairyland, part holiday. However, even in Shakespeare's time, May Day as an unchanging festival of national immortality, self-renewing like spring vegetation, was already a fantasy, and the Maygame a contested historical space. . . .

THE RITES OF MAY

Early on Midsummer's day, when Theseus and Hippolyta stumble across the four lovers sleeping in the woods, Theseus observes tactfully, "No doubt they rose up early to observe / The rite of May" (4.1.127–28). In *A Midsummer Night's Dream*, Shakespeare blends elements of two popular holidays, May Day and Midsummer's Eve, which, though six weeks apart, were not distinct occasions as holidays are in our Hallmark times. Instead, Maygames were celebrated throughout the months of May and June, and the two holidays overlapped, encompassing the whole season of warm weather, long days, fertility, and growth. How were the rites of May performed? Since a defining feature of popular culture is the absence of written records, to imagine these practices we must rely on the observations and descriptions of the literate elite. . . .

The "bringing home of May" is recorded as early as 1240, but the Maygame performed throughout the spring and early summer, believed to have been a hybrid of ancient urban festivals and agricultural celebrations superimposed with the feast days of the Christian calendar, took shape in the fifteenth and sixteenth centuries. May Day, perhaps an offshoot of the Roman Floralia and Celtic vernal festivals, had become the feast of Saints Philip and James, and Midsummer Day, the summer solstice marked in Roman times by a feast of the household gods, was celebrated as the feast day of St. John the Baptist. As Christian celebrations, the holidays retained the imprint of agricultural origins, with spring fertility incarnated in the green-leafed branches carried home from the forest and the floral Maypole erected on the common, and the growth season of long, sunny days honored by the fires and watches of St. John's Eve.

On May Day, the return of spring was celebrated with a collective return to the woods at daybreak to gather branches of sycamore and hawthorn to trim doorways, church, and street, and to collect the Maydew believed to confer eternal beauty. On the village green, a tree or bush was adorned or a flower-decked Maypole set up around which the celebrants joyfully danced. A Puck-like Lord of Misrule (sometimes in the person of Robin Hood, seasonally attired in green or yellow) played tricks on the revelers, a feast sponsored by parish or town was hosted by a Lord and Lady of May, a procession of musicians and morris dancers enlivened the proceedings, and a play might be performed. Since May Day was a fertility feast and therefore a suitable occasion for sexual license, sooner or later young women might return from the woods wearing grass-stained "green gowns."

If May Day celebrated the natural world and the light of day, Midsummer's Eve celebrated the supernatural and the night. Midsummer's Eve was a time of fantasy, magic, and heat-driven madness, when apparitions could be summoned foretelling marriage and death. Monstrous shapes danced by the light of bonfires, sometimes made of bones since the resulting stench was thought to banish evil spirits. In London, elaborate torchlight processions wound through the city, with "great and ugly giants marching as if they were alive, and armed at all points, but within . . . stuffed full of brown paper and tow [hemp fibers], which the shrewd boys underpeering [did] guilefully discover and turn to great derision" ([George] Puttenham). Flowers with magical properties like St. John's wort were gathered by young women and carefully arrayed for the purposes of bewitchment or prophecy, and in the woods, couples performing the rites of May might encounter fairies dancing in rounds on green meadows, pinching untidy maids in their sleep, or misleading poor travelers.

EVOKING THE FESTIVE SPIRIT

In *A Midsummer Night's Dream*, these vernal festivals are not, of course, pedantically reconstructed point by point, although fairies do dance in rounds and travelers are misled. Instead, familiar images flicker "momentary as a sound, / Swift as a shadow, short as any dream" (1.1.143–44) and vanish as soon as they are glimpsed. In the spirit of festive inversion, the play upends traditional customs: May was the time of female fertility over which the moon presided, but the play begins with an image of lunar age and sterility, a "dowager," a "cold fruitless moon" (1.1.5,73). The young lovers Hermia and Lysander set out not *to* the romantic May Day wood but *through* it to the barren domicile of Lysander's spinster aunt (1.1.157–60). Oberon and Titania, kindred of the cheerful and sunny Lord and Lady of May, are "ill met by moonlight" (2.1.60). Bottom is "translated" to a hobbyhorse (3.1.97), which traditionally accompanied the morris dancers, and Robin Hood's arrows to Cupid's fiery shafts. The "Painted Maypole" that traditionally signified male fertility becomes an epithet of ill-favored femininity hurled at Helena by an angry Hermia (3.2.296), and the magical Maydew that made ladies beautiful is replaced by the enchanting fairy juice that makes Oberon powerful (2.1.166–85). These dream-like fragments of popular holiday practices in *A Midsummer Night's Dream* are not merely festive play with "antique fables," but evoke the play's "local habitation," a society in the midst of radical cultural transformation.

In *A Survey of London,* John Stow offers accounts of the Maygame and the Midsummer Watch that emphasize the merriment, harmony, richness, and variety of these traditional celebrations in the City of London. Stow's London is a model of hierarchy and civic rule in which the social conflicts of his day are reduced to "warlike shows," and holidays are a fantasy of medieval hospitality that erases the contemporary spectre of dearth with vigil tables "furnished with sweet bread and good drink, and meats and drinks plentifully." His vigorous, confident portrait of festive London confirms the image of England as a fruitful commonwealth whose birthright is concord and order—an image that has endured far longer than the festivals he described, and informed later notions of English festivity. . . .

PROTESTANT OUTRAGE

If conservatives like Stow envisioned the festivals of the past as a socially beneficial model of harmony, order, and generosity, and a personally salutary celebration of good fellowship and forgiveness, for Puritans like Stubbes, holiday practices shredded the social fabric, substituted pleasure for godliness, and encouraged wickedness. Up to a point, the reformists were correct: May Day was potentially dangerous. On a designated "independence day," in the relative seclusion of the woods beyond familial and civic control, more than sexual liberties might be taken, and May Day had long been associated with rebellion and youthful violence.

Although many Protestant extremists were outraged by the old holiday practices, opposition to festivity was neither consistent nor uniformly observed, for the reformist movement included moderate Anglicans as well as stringent Puritans, and the latter included gentry and merchants as well as craftsmen and the poor. According to the extremists, dancing was "an introduction to whoredom, a preparative to wantonness, a provocative to uncleanness, an entry to all kind of lewdness" (Stubbes), but many Protestants, like the earl of Leicester, danced anyway. Most likely, popular holidays inspired a variety of sentiments in addition to pleasure or outrage, including, perhaps, indifference or irritation. However, Stow's nostalgic descriptions and Stubbes's acrimonious ones convey the wide range of attitudes toward holiday pastimes and the social divisions that these attitudes articulated and intensified.

Actors and Audiences

Alvin B. Kernan

A Midsummer Night's Dream features a play-within-a-play in its last act, and the lower class "mechanicals" who rehearse this play raise persistent questions about the nature of acting and the expectations of theater audiences. When these men actually stage their production, their audience must consider the role played by imagination in sustaining theatrical illusion. A Mellon Professor of the Humanities at Princeton University, Alvin B. Kernan examines these issues in the context of the rise of professional acting companies in Shakespeare's day and the changing composition of theater audiences.

The English drama of the Renaissance has for so long been thought of in Romantic terms as the highest of the high arts, the glory of Literature, that it is now difficult to understand in what low esteem plays and stage were held during the great dramatic period in England from the building of the first professional playhouse in London in 1576 to the closing of the theaters by the Puritans in 1642. It was not that drama itself was despised, for the Roman dramatists, and to a lesser degree the Greeks, were studied, admired, translated, imitated, and performed in aristocratic and academic settings. Drama was widely understood, except by the more radical Puritans, who abominated all playing as pagan pretense and idleness, to be a high art with a long tradition of greatness in presenting moral truths and advising princes in memorable and powerful ways.

The theater that was despised, feared, and mocked was a professional theater which evolved during the sixteenth century from mummings and agricultural festivals, the old biblical cycles and public pageants, juggling acts and morality plays, morris dances and courtly entertainments. Professional acting companies formed during the fifteenth century

Excerpted from Alvin B. Kernan, *The Playwright as Magician: Shakespeare's Image of the Poet.* Copyright © 1979. Reprinted with permission from Yale University Press.

and toured the country, playing on trestle stages in inn yards and public squares, before the screen in great halls of noble houses and guildhalls, in churches and in chapter houses. . . .

With the construction in 1576, just to the north of the London wall, of the first of many permanent playhouses, the public theater began to stabilize in London—though the companies were still forced frequently to tour—with daily performances, distinguished star actors, professional playwrights, and a more solid financial base. . . .

The control of the actors over their plays was ultimately almost absolute. The acting company commissioned the plays, paying on the average about six pounds in the 1590s, which, as Gerald Bentley points out, was a fairly good wage when ten pounds was a schoolmaster's annual wage and forty shillings the usual payment by a printer for a book. Later the rate rose to as high as twenty pounds, but even in the 1590s a busy playwright could make twenty to thirty pounds a year. . . .

A NEW KIND OF AUDIENCE

Dramatists thus found themselves in a new economic and artistic status as writers for wages, or as entrepreneurs who produced goods for the entertainment marketplace and depended for a living on the saleability of their commodity. It was difficult to think of what they produced under these circumstances as art expressing a poet's genius and winning him eternal fame by its perfect and permanent form. Instead, the actual facts of production defined plays as an amusement product, written on commission, often put together in collaboration, shaped to the styles and interests of particular actors, constantly changing form in the theater, used up in production, and dependent on pleasing for a moment the tastes of "Dukes and ambassadors, gentlemen and captains, citizens and apprentices, ruffians and harlots, 'Tailers, Tinkers, Cordwayners, Saylers, olde Men, yong Men, Women, Boyes, Girles, and such like'" [Stephen Gosson].

It was this audience on which the income of the theaters and of the playwrights depended, and no poets had previously faced and had to please a large public of this particular kind and with this degree of power over art. The courtly poet had purposely limited his audience to a small, select group, and the new professional poets of the latter sixteenth century, like Spenser or Donne, had also addressed only a patron and a small circle of men with similar aristocratic tastes. But the English playwrights now found themselves paid and judged by a group very different from the small intellectual and social world which had previously been the audience for art. . . .

Whatever the exact nature of the audience may have been—and the evidence suggests that it was far more likely to have been a cross-section of London, with a predominance of educated and intelligent people than "a broode of Hellbred creatures" [Henry Crosse, 1603]—there is no question that Shakespeare pleased it with plays that only rarely pandered to low or debased tastes. We know this not only from the fact that he prospered and became a rich man from his involvement with the theater, but also from the contemporary tributes paid him as the greatest and most popular of the English playwrights. A real sense of his popularity and the excitement that the plays created in the theater can be felt in the lines Leonard Digges wrote for inclusion in the 1640 edition of Shakespeare's poems:

> So have I seene, when Cesar would appeare,
> And on the Stage at half-sword parley were,
> *Brutus* and *Cassius:* Oh how the Audience
> Were ravish'd, with what wonder they went thence, . . .
>   let but Falstaffe come,
> *Hall, Poines,* the rest you scarce shall have a roome
> All is so pester'd: let but *Beatrice*
> And *Benedicke* be seene, loe in a trice
> The Cockpit Galleries, Boxes, all are full
> To heare *Maluoglio* that crosse garter'd Gull.

Shakespeare was remarkable among the playwrights of the time for the close relationship he maintained with his fellow actors in the company which produced his plays, and for the popularity he enjoyed with his large audience from early on in his career. But his success in dealing with these two new and crucial factors in the creation of art did not apparently make him any the less wary of them or the less concerned about the part they had to play in the theater if his plays were to achieve the effects he conceived as being within the possibility of great dramatic art. References in his plays to actors and to acting are on balance negative, and the audiences he portrays on stage are never ideal but always something less than satisfactory in their behavior and their comprehension. Of all the English dramatists, Shakespeare seems to have been torn most severely between the conception of his plays as high art and as mere entertainment, and Philip Edwards rightly calls him "the experimenter, engaged in a continuous battle, a quarter of a century long, against his own skepticism about the value of his art as a model of human experience." He left us no direct critical statements about the issue, of course, but instead explored the question in his plays by allowing his characters and his scenes to state and to pose again and again the fundamental theatrical problems. His concerns and his developing understanding of the theater are imaged most sharply and summarily in the little internal plays, the plays-within-the-play, which, as Leslie Fiedler puts it, allow a play to provide "a history of itself, a record of the scruples and the hesitations of its maker in the course of its making, sometimes even a defense or definition of the kind to which it belongs or the conventions which it respects." Shakespeare's scruples and hesitations

THE ANXIETY OF THE MECHANICALS

Though Duke Theseus demonstrates a tolerant attitude toward the mechanicals and their play, there is also considerable tension between the upper and lower classes in A Midsummer Night's Dream. *This tension, as Theodore Leinwand observes, is most obvious in the mechanicals' fear of punishment if they should frighten the ladies with their play.*

Negotiation, arbitration, and accommodation characterize Bottom's and his fellow artisans' relations with their social superiors. It is often remarked that the artisans betray a most naive understanding of the theater. Their discussions in I.ii and in III.i revolve around technical problems, obstacles that may prevent them from convincing their audience. But their specific fears are resonant because they have to do with more than theatrical decorum. In particular, the players are anxious not to "fright the Duchess and the ladies" (I.ii.70–71) with their lion, or to seem to do harm with their swords (III.i.17). The artisans do not want to strike fear into the hearts of their social betters; indeed, such a reaction "were enough to hang us all." "That would hang us, every mother's son" (I.ii.73), they chorus together. To "draw a sword" is to cause "a parlous fear" (III.i.10,11), and such a fear can only cost the crew their lives. They fear for their lives because they assume that indecorous actions on their part will cause their spectators to fear for *their* lives. Bottom knows that "If you think I come hither as a lion, it about the effect of actors and audiences on his plays are focused in three of his early plays, *The Taming of the Shrew*, *Love's Labour's Lost*, and *A Midsummer Night's Dream*, where internal plays are staged in such a way as to reveal the nature of the doubts a practicing playwright had about the ability of actors to present, and audiences to understand and be properly moved by, the poet's "most rare vision.". . .

THE LIMITATIONS OF ACTORS AND AUDIENCES

In his first decade as a dramatist, Shakespeare seems to have been on the whole optimistic about the power of playing to affect, even in less than ideal circumstances, the real world. He laughs at actors for their clumsiness and audiences for their literal-mindedness, chiding both for their inability to forget themselves and enter fully into the play; but the laughter, while it bears witness to some uneasiness on the part of the dramatist about his theater, seems in many ways

were pity of my life" (III.i.40–41). And Bottom's fear is not his alone. "Lion" takes Bottom's advice and announces that he is but Snug the joiner. He then reveals his anxiety, borrowing Bottom's very words: *"For if I should as lion come in strife / Into this place, 'twere pity on my life"* (V.i.220–221).

The relationship that the artisans think they have with their superiors and the attitude that they assume their superiors have toward them betray considerable anxiety. Swords, fear of hanging, and strife are a part of this interaction from first to last act. Given the players' fear of potential retribution, there is something uncannily appropriate to Theseus' response to their play: "Never excuse; for when the players are all dead, there need none to be blamed. Marry, if he that writ it had played Pyramus, and hanged himself in Thisbe's garter, it would have been a fine tragedy. . ." (V.i.342–346). The players fear for their lives, and their audience jests them into oblivion. Bottom tells Snug to announce, "I am a man, as other men are" (III.i.42–43); but during the performance, Demetrius jests that Bottom is "Less than an ace, man; for he is dead, he is nothing" (V.i.297). Performance, especially strife- and sword-filled performance, is potentially life threatening in the world of *A Midsummer Night's Dream*. No wonder Starveling opines, "I believe we must leave the killing out, when all is done" (III.i.13–14).

Theodore B. Leinwand, "'I Believe We Must Leave the Killing Out': Deference and Accommodation in *A Midsummer Night's Dream*," in *Renaissance Papers 1986*. Durham, NC: Southeastern Renaissance Conference, 1986.

merely the graceful modesty of an accomplished and self-assured professional dramatic poet continuing the proud humanistic tradition of claiming high value for his theatrical art. Nowhere is the modesty so complete, and at the same time the claim for the potential value of playing so extensive, as in *A Midsummer Night's Dream*, where Shakespeare dramatizes Sidney's boast that in place of nature's brazen world the poet creates a golden one, that imagination can perceive and art reveal an unseen reality just beyond the range of the senses and of the rational mind. In the *Dream*, art is no longer defined only by its ability to shape and transform an obstinate reality, as in *Shrew* and *Love's Labour's Lost*, but is shown to have an ability to penetrate the screen of the immediate world and reveal an imaginative truth that lies behind it.

Again Shakespeare glances, with an amusement that still betrays uneasiness, at the crudities of actors and stage and at the limitations of audiences. No players could be more hopeless than Nick Bottom the weaver and his mechanical friends who, in the hope of winning a small pension, perform the internal play, "Pyramus and Thisbe," to celebrate the marriage of Duke Theseus of Athens to the Amazon queen, Hippolyta. Bottom's company, a parody of the amateur players and provincial touring companies who performed in aristocratic houses on special occasions, is so literal-minded as to require that the moon actually shine on the stage, that the wall through which Pyramus and Thisbe speak be solidly there, and that the actor who plays the lion assure the ladies in the audience, lest they be afraid, that he is only a make-believe lion. The deficiency of imagination which lies behind such a laughable conception of theater, carries over into the playing style of the actors as well. Their stumbling rant, missed cues, mispronounced words and lines, willingness to converse directly with the audience, doggerel verse, and general ineptitude, constitute a playwright's nightmare and completely destroy any possibility of creating the necessary illusion. . . .

The audience at "Pyramus and Thisbe," Duke Theseus, his queen Hippolyta, and the young lovers who attend them, are socially superior to the actors but little more sophisticated about their proper roles in making a play work. Theseus does understand that, though this may be "the silliest stuff" ever heard, it lies within the power of a gracious audience to improve it, for "The best in this kind are but shadows; and the worst are no worse, if imagination amend them" (5.1.211–12). But the noble audience seems to have little of the necessary imagination, for they violate the imaginative space of the play, which the players have first breached, by mocking the actors, laughing at their tragic efforts, and talking loudly among themselves during the performance. For them a play is only the means to while away a dull wait on their wedding night and, secure in an untroubled sense of their own substantial reality, they can laugh at what unrealistic and trivial things all plays and players are. Theseus, that champion of Athenian rationalism, has already publicly declared that the poet's imagination is no more truthful than the lunatic's delusions or the lover's belief in the perfect beauty of his beloved:

> The poet's eye, in a fine frenzy rolling,
> Doth glance from heaven to earth, from earth to heaven;
> And as imagination bodies forth
> The forms of things unknown, the poet's pen
> Turns them to shapes, and gives to airy nothing
> A local habitation and a name
>
> [5.1.12-17]

Shakespeare seems to have constructed in *Dream* the "worst case" for theater, voicing all the attacks on drama being made in his time and deliberately showing plays, actors, and audiences at their worst. And since "the best in this kind are but shadows," "Pyramus and Thisbe" seems to indict all plays, including *A Midsummer Night's Dream,* as mere rant of awkward actors and unrealistic dreaming of frenzied poets. But, while admitting the worst, Shakespeare has contrived at the same time to defend plays in a most subtle fashion. Even as Theseus and his friends sit watching "Pyramus and Thisbe," laughing at poetry and plays and actors, they are themselves, seen from our vantage point in the outer audience, only the "forms of things unknown" which the imagination of William Shakespeare bodied forth and gave the habitation of Athens and such odd names as Helena and Hermia, Demetrius and Lysander. The situation is the same as that in *Love's Labour's Lost,* where the scorn for plays is also discredited by showing the audience to be themselves only players, and not such very good ones at that, in a larger play of which they are totally unaware.

This is true in *Dream* in the literal sense that the stage audience is made up of actors in Shakespeare's play, and also in the sense that they have already been unwitting players in another internal play written and produced by that master of illusion, Oberon, king of the fairies. He and Titania between them have earlier managed the lives of Theseus and Hippolyta as if they were unconscious actors in a play, and during the course of *Dream*, Oberon contrives on the stage of his magical forest a little illusion which instructs the young lovers, feelingly not consciously, in the dangers of unleashed passion and brings them at last to a happy conclusion in which every Jack has his Jill. Oberon's magical forest is a perfect image of what a theater might ideally be and do, but even here the most all-powerful of playwrights is subject to the ability of the imperfect instruments through whom he must implement his art, and Puck nearly ruins the play by putting "idleness" in the wrong eyes.

ALL THE WORLD A PLAY

As we in the audience watch Theseus watching Bottom pretend to be Pyramus, the extended dramatic perspective forces us to consider the possibility that we too may be only another player audience on another larger stage. And if this is the case, then the audience is not only once again reminded by the bad manners of the stage audience of the positive part it must play in making theater work, but it is also being told that its own sense of the real may be no more valid than Theseus's. If his rationalistic scorn of plays and players is called into question by his status as only another player, then perhaps our skepticism about Shakespeare's play is equally compromised, for we stand in the same relationship to the things unknown that the imagination of William Shakespeare has bodied forth as *A Midsummer Night's Dream* as Theseus does to "Pyramus and Thisbe." A forest ruled over by a contentious fairy king and queen, a magical love potion which causes love at first sight, a comic trickster like Puck, all are at least as real as a player duke who marries a queen of Amazons, rules over a city named Athens, and believes that a way of thinking called reason shows the truth of things. And they may finally be as real as that "sure and firm-set earth" we take to be our own reality. If *all* the world is a play, then one play may be as true as another; and if the conditions are right, as in Oberon's play but not in Bottom's, then the theater may reveal the true nature of the world and effect its transformation.

The playwright drives home his point in the final scene. After Theseus and Hippolyta and the other couples, Bottom's play finished, make their way to bed thinking that reality reigns again, the stage fills with all those fairies which Shakespeare's imagination created to embody his vision of the beneficent but tricky forces at work in nature, just beyond the range of the daylight eye. Again it is done lightly, the claim half concealed and discounted even as it is so charmingly made, but immediate reality is being heavily discounted and a visionary power is being claimed for the dramatic poet by leaving his fairies in possession of a stage which now extends outward to claim the entire theater and the world beyond as a part of its imaginative realm.

The Fairy World

John Russell Brown

Most people in Shakespeare's day were inclined to believe in supernatural creatures such as elves, sprites, and fairies, according to Shakespeare scholar and editor John Russell Brown. Brown contends that Shakespeare uses such nonhuman beings as outward expressions of his characters' inner fears, desires, and other subconscious states. The fairies of the play are agents of transformation and represent the power of imagination and its central role in love.

Belief in fairies is rare in our times, even among the smallest children, but Shakespeare's *A Midsummer Night's Dream*, which is presided over by Oberon and Titania, King and Queen of fairies, and which is full of magic and enchantment, is still read and performed throughout the world. The reason is that the fairies in this play are not simply a self-contained, miniature, and pretty tribe of creatures, not unlike human beings but usually invisible to mortal eyes. Shakespeare saw them like that in his mind's eye, and yet as much more besides.

Most of Shakespeare's contemporaries did believe that there were spirits of all sorts alive in the world and existing in its various elements of earth, air, fire, and water. They called them many different names, such as sprites, goblins, daemons, devils, elves, spirits, creatures, and fairies. Water-devils or naiads were sometimes called fairies; according to some authorities, they had a queen and

> cause inundations, many times shipwrecks, and deceive men in diverse ways, as *succubae* or otherwise, appearing most part in women's shapes. . .

That is Robert Burton's account in *The Anatomy of Melancholy,* first published in 1621 and drawing together the opinions of many former writers. Spirits living in earth included "lares, genii, fauns, satyres, wood-nymphs, foliots, fairies, Robin Goodfellows, trolls." Burton recalled how these have

Excerpted from John Russell Brown, "Introduction," in *A Midsummer Night's Dream*, by William Shakespeare. Copyright © 1996 by Applause Books. Reprinted with permission from Applause Books.

been in former times adored with much superstition, with sweeping their houses, and setting a pail of clean water, good victuals and the like. . . These are they that dance on heaths and greens.

Sometimes they would lead mortals to their hiding-places and show them marvelous sights. Paracelsus, a renowned German scholar of the early sixteenth century, reported that they had been seen walking in little coats, some two foot long. Ludwig Lavater, whose treatise *Of Ghosts and Spirits Walking by Night* was translated into English in 1572, said that these pucks or pooks "draw men out of the way, and lead them all night a by-way, or quite bar them of their way."

IMAGINATION AND FAIRIES

But not every Elizabethan believed in fairies. The notes to Edmund Spenser's early poem, *The Shepheard's Calendar* (1579), are forthright in condemning such superstition:

> the opinion of fairies and elves is very old, and yet sticketh very religiously in the minds of some. But to root that rank opinion of elves out of men's hearts, the truth is that there be no such things, nor yet the shadows of the things.

Such absolute dissent was not common however, for while doubts were often expressed about the actual existence of these spirits, it was a most respectable opinion that men could *imagine* that they saw such creatures. This idea is crucial for understanding Shakespeare's use of fairies and of many other magic and supernatural events in the plays. His non-human beings are "shadows," or outward expressions of thoughts and feelings, the means to represent almost nameless fears and excitements, and almost intangible sensations.

Shakespeare's characters speak about fairies when their imaginations or fantasies are seething with possibilities and doubts, and with images which transcend or ignore the ordinary affairs of life. In *The Comedy of Errors*, Dromio of Syracuse arrives in Ephesus to find himself ordered about by a fine lady he has never seen before, so that he hardly knows what is happening and falls to his prayers: "O, for my beads! I cross me for a sinner!" But this changes nothing and he is precipitated towards superstitious fantasy:

> This is fairy land. O spite of spites!
> We talk with goblins, owls, and sprites.
> If we obey them not, this will ensue:
> They'll suck our breath, or pinch us black and blue.
> (II.ii.187–90)

He says, and his master agrees with him, that he has been
"transformed," altered out of all recognition by magic; he
believes that he has been changed into an "ass."

In *Romeo and Juliet*, Shakespeare's hero is unwilling to go
to a ball because he has had a bad dream. His friend, Mercutio, says at once that this is fairies' work:

> O then I see Queen Mab hath been with you.
> She is the fairies' midwife, and she comes
> In shape no bigger than an agate stone
> On the fore-finger of an alderman,
> Drawn with a team of little atomies,
> Over men's noses as they lie asleep; . . . (I.iv.53–58)

Mercutio goes on to ascribe to Queen Mab the power to reflect the inward thoughts of all sorts of people, functioning
differently for each according to their preoccupations,
whether courtier, lawyer, lady, parson, soldier, or whatever.
When he starts to speak of young girls who dream of lovemaking, Romeo interrupts the flight of fantasy with

> Peace, peace, Mercutio, peace!
> Thou talk'st of nothing.

"True," comes the answer:

> I talk of dreams,
> Which are the children of an idle brain,
> Begot of nothing but vain fantasy. (I.iv.94–97)

The existence of fairies could be discussed seriously in
Shakespeare's day, but, like dreams, their credibility depended on the eye and mind of the beholder. At the close of
A Midsummer Night's Dream, Puck, who belongs to the
play's fairy kingdom and yet interferes often in mortal affairs, steps forward to say:

> If we shadows have offended,
> Think but this, and all is mended:
> That you have but slumb'red here
> While these visions did appear.
> And this weak and idle theme,
> No more yielding but a dream,
> Gentles, do not reprehend. (V.i.404–10)

Puck speaks of "shadows"—reflections of humankind, images, insubstantial beings, dark shapes attending substantial
bodies—the same word that is found in the notes of *The
Shepheard's Calendar*. When the lovers in the *Dream* wake
in the wood where they have been misled and enchanted by
Puck, Demetrius thinks everything has been a dream, and
still is a dream:

> Are you sure
> That we are awake? It seems to me
> That yet we sleep, we dream. (IV.i.188–90)

This is exactly what Puck asks the audience to think, and
what Oberon had foretold: the mortals would

> think no more of this night's accidents
> But as the fierce vexation of a dream. (IV.i.64–65)

The King of fairies seems unaware that some of his victims
would find their dream to be sweet or wonderful, and "past
the wit of man to say what dream it was" (IV.i.201–02).

Shakespeare's association of dreams and fairies was fully
in accord with renaissance psychology. The inward senses
were thought to be of three kinds: common sense, fantasy,
and memory. "Fantasy" is that capacity of mind which can
cause a person to think he or she sees strange, monstrous,
and absurd things when these do not actually exist and have
no objective reality. Although most active when dreaming,
fantasy can dominate consciousness whenever the hold of
"common sense" (or "reason") is relaxed and so fails to exercise its usual control. The "seething brains" of lovers, as
they are called in this play, were said to be among the most
apt to imagine that they see fantastic and unreal sights, and
to believe that they have been transported to strange worlds
or transformed into new shapes. When learned men debated
whether love was seated in the heart, liver, or fantasy, they
usually pronounced in favor of the fantasy, or, as some
would say, the imagination.

THE POWER OF IMAGINATION

A Midsummer Night's Dream is about fairies and enchantment, but, more than this, it is a comedy about the imagination. Much of its action takes place at night when fantasy is
most active. Its human characters are seized by love, anger, or
ambition; some are the prey of fairies and act in the strangest
and most headlong ways, and others of their own free will en-
act a fantastic play about heroic love. When the lovers have es-
caped from the enchanted wood and are prepared for marriage, Duke Theseus, who is himself a bridegroom,
recognizes the truth of the strange events he has been told, not
because he believes in fairies but because it is true to his experience of what lovers, lunatics, and poets can imagine:

> Lovers and madmen have such seething brains,
> Such shaping fantasies, that apprehend

> More than cool reason ever comprehends.
> The lunatic, the lover and the poet
> Are of imagination all compact.
> One sees more devils than vast hell can hold;
> That is the madman. The lover, all as frantic,
> Sees Helen's beauty in a brow of Egypt.
> The poet's eye, in a fine frenzy rolling,
> Doth glance from heaven to earth, from earth to heaven;
> And as imagination bodies forth
> The forms of things unknown, the poet's pen
> Turns them to shapes and gives to airy nothing
> A local habitation and a name.
> Such tricks hath strong imagination
> That, if it would but apprehend some joy,
> It comprehends some bringer of that joy;
> Or in the night, imagining some fear,
> How easy is a bush supposed a bear! (V.i.4–22)

The lovers and the fairies of the *Dream* use similar verbal images, and act with similar speed, lightness, changeability, and unreflecting cruelty, and the play's poet-dramatist seems to have been equally at home with both groups of characters.

The supernatural characters of the play are not of any strict lineage. Oberon and Titania inhabit the world of classical myth and are thus associated with the power of natural phenomena. Through their "distemperature" we see

> The seasons alter: hoary-headed frosts
> Fall in the fresh lap of the crimson rose,
> And on old Hiems' thin and icy crown
> An odorous chaplet of sweet summer buds
> Is, as in mockery, set. (II.i.107–11)

But they are also denizens of the English countryside and, with their troops of followers, they quarrel, dance, and process through green woods and flowery fields. Their servants hang dewdrops in cowslips' ears and steal light from glowworms and the painted wings of butterflies. These more domestic functions belong to a folk tradition, derided by King James in his treatise on *Daemonology* (1597):

> How there was a King and Queen of fairy, of such a jolly court and train as they had; how they had a tend [or tythe] and duty, as it were, of all goods; how they naturally rode and went, ate and drank, and did all other actions like natural men and women.

Yet Oberon and Titania outstep this tradition too, being more than self-concerned: they also attend the nuptials of mortals and wish blessings on them, as spirits of fecundity have

done according to folklore in many countries across the
world. More than this, they inhabit the elegant and golden
world of pastoral poetry:

> And in the shape of Corin sat all day,
> Playing on pipes of corn and versing love
> To amorous Philida. (II.i.66–68)

In this guise they represent a dream of simplicity and fulfill-
ment.

Puck, or Robin Goodfellow as he is also called, stands out
from the other fairies in the *Dream* by being in a more
clearly rustic and domestic folk tradition, as he explains on
his first entrance (see II.i.34–57). He enjoys mere pranks,
and the waste of merry hours. But he also has other shapes,
attending Oberon dutifully and chasing the "rude mechanicals" out of the wood in the appearance of frightening monsters:

> Sometime a horse I'll be, sometime a hound,
>   A hog, a headless bear, sometime a fire;
> And neigh, and bark, and grunt, and roar, and burn,
>   Like horse, hound, hog, bear, fire, at every turn.
>   (III.i.94–97)

What is common to all Shakespeare's supernatural characters is not a consistent other-world which they inhabit, but
rather their ability to express the teeming richness and cap-
tivating power of human imagination. Bottom, the weaver,
who is snatched precipitously into the loving care of Titania,
experiences the most tender, exquisite, and harmonious
fairy love:

> I'll give thee fairies to attend on thee,
> And they shall fetch thee jewels from the deep,
> And sing while thou on pressed flowers dost sleep;
> And I will purge thy mortal grossness so,
> That thou shalt like an airy spirit go. (III.i.137–41)

Later the Queen of fairies takes Bottom in her arms:

> So doth the woodbine the sweet honeysuckle
> Gently entwist; the female ivy so
> Enrings the barky fingers of the elm.

And she concludes like a mortal lover, herself overwhelmed
with the new experience, almost at a loss for words:

> O how I love thee! How I dote on thee! (IV.i.38–41)

Bottom attempts to respond in a courtly manner, but soon he
complains of itches and hunger, and then falls asleep. . . . But
when Bottom wakes from his "dream," something remains

in his fuddled brain, a wonder that shatters all normal understanding. To express this consciousness, Shakespeare gives to his clumsy but adventurous weaver the words that St. Paul had used in speaking of the love of God. In the Bishops' Bible, Shakespeare's contemporaries would read that

> The eye hath not seen, and the ear hath not heard, neither have entered into the heart of man, the things which God hath prepared for them that love him. (*I Corinthians*, II.9)

What Bottom says is:

> The eye of man hath not heard, the ear of man hath not seen, man's hand is not able to taste, his tongue to conceive, nor his heart to report, what my dream was. (IV.i.206–09)

He cannot describe his fairy experience, except insofar as he had been an ass; but his fantasy retains a glimmering sense of wonder, glory, and humility, because in some sense the dream was his own.

When the play's action leaves the wood and returns to Athens, Shakespeare still has not finished with his exploration of imaginative reality. As the uncultured "mechanicals" struggle to perform their uncouth and lofty play, growing in self-confidence and absurdity, Theseus and his queen come to realise the extent to which imaginative involvement can find a response and justification only by an answering imaginative acceptance:

> HIPPOLYTA: This is the silliest stuff that ever I heard.
> THESEUS: The best in this kind are but shadows; and the worst are no worse, if imagination amend them.
> HIPPOLYTA: It must be your imagination then, and not theirs.
> THESEUS: If we imagine no worse of them than they of themselves, they may pass for excellent men. Here come two noble beasts in, a man and a lion.   (V.i.206–12)

The opposite—the exposure and pain which an unequal response can bring—is shown as Starveling, enacting the role of Moonshine, is mocked and humiliated by the young lovers. This audience can catch no resemblance between their fantasies and that which the stumbling actor attempts to display.

When Puck holds the stage to speak an epilogue, after the players have danced off stage and the lovers have gone to bed, he offers the audience an awareness of their own mortality, beyond any previous fantasy in the comedy:

> Now the hungry lion roars,
>   And the wolf behowls the moon;

Whilst the heavy plowman snores,
    All with weary task fordone.
Now the wasted brands do glow,
    Whilst the screech owl, screeching loud,
Puts the wretch that lies in woe
    In remembrance of a shroud... (V.i.352–59)

After this dark moment, the fairies reenter in procession, carrying lights and singing, and the various imaginative transformations of *A Midsummer Night's Dream* end in delight.

The Play's Depiction of Female Power

Helen Hackett

Scholars generally agree that one of Oberon's speeches in *A Midsummer Night's Dream* functions as praise of Queen Elizabeth; in this, Shakespeare participates in a literary practice widespread during the later decades of Elizabeth's reign. British scholar Helen Hackett, however, contends that other aspects of the play—the subjugation of Hippolyta and the degradation of Titania—directly challenge the notion of female rule and female power. Hackett suggests that this critical treatment may echo some of the widespread discontent with female rule during the last decade of Elizabeth's life.

A Midsummer Night's Dream can be dated to 1595–6; it thus belongs to the final decade of the reign of Elizabeth I, who died in 1603. Moon-imagery was extremely common in the literature of this decade, especially in panegyric (that is, the literature of praise and celebration of the monarch). Diana, goddess of chastity, was obviously a fitting persona for the Virgin Queen, an aptness reinforced by the fact that Elizabeth's favourite pastime was hunting. The moon could also, as ruler of the tidal oceans, be adopted as a symbol of England's burgeoning imperial aspirations. For example, in 1591, during a royal progress, entertainments were provided for the Queen and her court at Elvetham; they included marine pageants on a pool constructed in the shape of a crescent moon, and Elizabeth was hailed as 'Fair Cynthia the wide Ocean's Empress.'

George Peele, in *The Honour of the Garter,* 1593, represents the procession of the Queen and the Knights of the Garter at Windsor as a dream-vision of the rising moon and stars in the night sky:

Under the glorious spreading wings of Fame,
I saw a Virgin Queen, attired in white,
Leading with her a sort of goodly knights

. . . .
She was the sovereign of the knights she led.
Her face methought I knew: as if the same,
The same great Empress that we here enjoy,
Had climbed the clouds, and been in person there;
To whom the earth, the sea, and elements
Auspicious are.

The poem demonstrates why moon-imagery became so
prevalent in panegyric: it rendered Elizabeth ethereal, radiant and quasi-divine. Similarly, George Chapman, in *The
Shadow of Night*, 1594, represented Elizabeth as the rising
moon-goddess, 'Enchantress-like, decked in disparent
lawn, / Circled with charms and incantations.'

Such poetic visions are closely echoed in Act II of *A Midsummer Night's Dream*, when Oberon describes to Puck his
vision of an 'imperial vot'ress' whose invulnerability to Cupid's arrow resulted in the transformation of the flower into
a love-charm. He recounts:

I saw, but thou couldst not,
Flying between the cold moon and the earth
Cupid, all armed. A certain aim he took
At a fair vestal thronèd by the west,
And loosed his love-shaft smartly from his bow
As it should pierce a hundred thousand hearts.
But I might see young Cupid's fiery shaft
Quenched in the chaste beams of the wat'ry moon,
And the imperial vot'ress passèd on,
In maiden meditation, fancy-free.

(II. i. 155–64)

The terms 'vestal', 'thronèd by the west', and 'imperial', combined with the association with the chaste moon, were all conventional to poetic representations of Elizabeth, and clearly indicate that this passage participates in contemporary royal
panegyric. Just like Peele's and Chapman's moon-goddesses,
this superhuman figure glides translucently across the sky.

At another point in Chapman's poem, he exhorted the regal moon-goddess:

Ascend thy chariot, and make earth admire
Thy old swift changes, made a young fixed prime;
O let thy beauty scorch the wings of time.

Here we see a further reason why lunar imagery became increasingly popular for Elizabeth in the 1590s: as she grew

older, its cyclical connotations could be used to suggest powers of infinite self-renewal, infinite youthfulness, and even goddess-like immortality. A song in praise of the Queen published in John Dowland's *Third Book of Songs*, 1603, declared:

> See the moon
> That ever in one change doth grow
> Yet still the same; and she is so;
> So, so, so, and only so.

THE DECLINE OF ELIZABETH

However, these celebrations of Elizabeth's immunity to change and mortality were of course idealizations, and there is other evidence that as the 1590s progressed she was visibly in decline. She was in her sixties, and as her public image in portraiture as well as poetry became ever more perfect and idealized, a 'mask of youth', it was increasingly removed from, and arguably compensatory for, her ageing physical reality. A gathering consciousness of the imminence of her death, combined with the fact that the end of the century was near, gave an acute sense of impending transition, a feeling that the present era was waning and would shortly give way to a new start. On the one hand the prospect of change seems to have induced some anxiety and uncertainty; after all, most of Elizabeth's subjects had been born since her accession in 1558—including Shakespeare, born in 1564—and had therefore never known another monarch. On the other hand, though, there was also excitement at the prospect of a new beginning, and feverish rumours of Elizabeth's illness and demise were rife for more than a decade before her death. This atmosphere created a widespread preoccupation with mutability—that is, the processes of change through time—which in turn gave impetus to the use of moon-imagery.

The eager anticipation of change was reinforced by the fact that Elizabeth's successor would be James of Scotland, returning England from what was, in terms of contemporary ideology and recent history, an anomalous and controversial state of rule by an unmarried and autonomous female, to the normal, 'natural' hierarchy which placed power in male hands. Bishop Goodman (1583–1656), looking back in later life on the last years of Elizabeth's reign, said that 'in effect the people were very generally weary of an old woman's government.' A favourite motif in elegies composed when Elizabeth

died was that of the feminine moon giving way to the more re-
splendent, masculine, dawning sun.

Impatience for change was compounded by various developing political discontents. At court, there was increasing
frustration with Elizabeth's perceived wilfulness and fickleness of favour, traits which were attributed to her age and
her femaleness. The more negative associations of the moon
with mutability and dubious female powers were not therefore excluded from lunar representations of Elizabeth, even
though, during her lifetime, they could of course only be in-
voked relatively indirectly. Her favourite Sir Walter Ralegh,
in a poem entitled *The Ocean to Cynthia*, probably composed
in 1592 when he was in severe disfavour, represents himself
as the ocean—Elizabeth had nicknamed him her 'Water'—
helplessly drawn in and out of favour by her moon-like
changeful influence. The poem begins as a celebration of
the Queen and a declaration of love for her, then darkens as
Ralegh complains of her arbitrary withdrawal of affection
and attributes it to the innate instability of womankind:

> So hath perfection which begat her mind
> Added thereto a change of fantasy,
> And left her the affections of her kind.

On top of Elizabeth's perceived fickleness towards individual courtiers, there was intense frustration with her cautious pragmatism in foreign policy and in government generally. Many of her younger male courtiers were impatient
to pursue military glory in the Netherlands, Ireland and the
New World. Her chief favourite of these later years, Robert
Devereux, Earl of Essex, told the French ambassador in 1597
that 'they laboured under two things at this Court, delay and
inconstancy, which proceeded chiefly from the sex of the
Queen.' It is hard not to be reminded by this of Theseus's impatience with the old moon; Elizabeth must have appeared
to Essex very much like an aged stepmother or dowager
constraining the full exercise of his virility while his youth
passed by. I do not mean to suggest by this that Theseus and
the old moon are direct allegorical personifications of Essex
and Elizabeth, but that a contemporary sense of female
power as an ageing and delaying force, as against male energy which chafes for action and progress, informs the gen-
dered lunar iconography of Theseus's lines. . . .

Moon-imagery was therefore invaluable to court poets of
the 1590s precisely because of its doubleness, the moon's

dark side as well as its radiant side, its changefulness as well as its infinite self-renewal. It could be used as a medium for what Annabel Patterson has called 'functional ambiguity': the expression of political criticism in coded terms, at once sufficiently veiled and ambivalent to evade the dangers of censorship and punishment, but at the same time soliciting the reader's implicit comprehension and collusion.

DISORDER IN SOCIETY

Ambivalence about female rule also extended beyond the court. The desire for a more aggressive, 'masculine' foreign policy was shared on a popular level, and can be detected in Shakespeare's *Henry V*, not least in the choral passage celebrating Essex's expected triumphant return from his military campaign in Ireland (Act V, ll. 29–34). In addition, the mid-1590s were a period of outbreaks of plague, failed harvests,

HIPPOLYTA'S SILENCE

For many years, it was assumed that Theseus's bride-to-be, Hippolyta, is cheerfully acquiescent in the play's first act. Recent interpretations and productions of the play have explored the different ways Hippolyta's silence may be understood. As scholar David Marshall suggests, Hippolyta's silence may be seen as a critique of the male authority of Egeus and Theseus as they control and "silence" Hermia, thwarting her choice in love.

Hippolyta stands as more than an ornament for a masque; her silence is an important key to the conflicts of *A Midsummer Night's Dream.* The problem of how to read her silence—and what it means to imagine what is going on behind the scenes, as it were, in the privacy of her mind—is one of the problems the play can teach us about. As readers who must imagine Hippolyta represented on a stage, we must first hear her silence; we must recognize that she does not speak. . . .

Hippolyta is not silent for the reasons that Cordelia [in *King Lear*] decides to "love, and be silent." Nor is she performing the "perfect ceremony of love's rite" in which one must "learn to read what silent love has writ." Hippolyta is, I believe, tongue-tied, as if she were the serious reflection of Bottom at the moment when Titania comically ravishes him with the command to her fairies: "Tie up my lover's tongue, bring him silently" (III, i, 186). Theseus (who has "heard" of Demetrius' food shortages, and inflation. Clearly, disease and failed crops were natural disasters, and could not be blamed on Elizabeth's rule; nevertheless, the privileges enjoyed by members of her court protected them from the consequences of those disasters, both in their ability to leave London for country estates when the plague struck, and in their possession of trade monopolies granted by the Crown which secured them from economic hardship at the expense of the poor. An Essex labourer in 1591, even before the worst period of deprivation, urged his fellow subjects to pray for a king, because 'the Queen is but a woman and ruled by noblemen, and the noblemen and gentlemen are all one, and the gentlemen and farmers will hold together so that the poor get nothing.'

Titania's speech about the cosmic reverberations of her conflict with Oberon may constitute a topical reference to the plague of 1593–4 and the exceptionally bad summer of

---

inconsistency but "being over-full of self-affairs" [I, i, 111–113] manages at least twice to forget about it) can therefore hear in Hippolyta's silence what he likes. He describes himself meeting frightened subjects who, unable to speak,

> dumbly have broke off,
> Not paying me a welcome. Trust me, sweet,
> Out of this silence yet I picked a welcome,
> And in the modesty of fearful duty
> I read as much as from the rattling tongue
> Of saucy and audacious eloquence.
> Love, therefore, and tongue-tied simplicity
> In least speak most, to my capacity.
>
> (V, i, 98–105)

These are noble sentiments; but if Hippolyta is tongue-tied (and she is silent after this speech as well), it does not necessarily follow that one should read love in her silence. Part of Theseus' judgment against Hermia's advocacy of her own will cites that she is "wanting [her] father's voice" (52); that is, she lacks her father's consent *and* she wants to speak in her father's voice, to speak with his authority. Theseus tells Hermia that her voice has no standing in his court; her appeal is overruled because her plea must fall on deaf ears. I suggest that both Hermia and Hippolyta are in effect tongue-tied in the same way: their fate is to have others dictate their sentiments while they are silent or silenced.

David Marshall, "Exchanging Visions: Reading *A Midsummer Night's Dream*," *ELH: English Literary History* 49:3 (Fall 1982): 543–575.

1594, as well as possibly the successive wet summers of
1595 and 1596:

> the green corn
> Hath rotted ere his youth attained a beard.
> . . . .
> The nine men's morris is filled up with mud,
> And the quaint mazes in the wanton green
> For lack of tread are undistinguishable.
> . . . .
> the moon, the governess of floods,
> Pale in her anger, washes all the air,
> That rheumatic diseases do abound.

(II. i. 94–5, 98–100, 103–5)

Simon Forman recorded in his journal for 1594 that

> June and July were very wet and wonderful cold like winter,
> [so] that the 10th day of July many did sit by the fire, it was so
> cold; and so was it in May and June. . . . There were many
> great floods this summer, and about Michaelmas, through
> the abundance of rain that fell suddenly.

Ernest Schanzer interprets Titania's speech in terms of the
Renaissance concepts of the macrocosm and microcosm: the
idea that the pattern, proportions and hierarchy of the universe
correspond to the pattern, proportions and hierarchy of humanity, such that levels of existence which are great and
small, or cosmic and local, are linked together by structures of
analogy. Hence disruption to the order of human society is
equivalent to a breach of natural order, and vice versa. For
Schanzer, then, Titania's speech is much more than just a topical allusion to bad weather; it is a description of 'disorder in
the macrocosm' which, as so often in Shakespeare, accompa-
nies and figures 'disorder in the body politic, here the state of
fairydom.' We may take this beyond the immediate world of
the play to draw connections with perceived disorder in the
body politic of Elizabeth's England. In Ralegh's *The Ocean to
Cynthia*, Elizabeth as moon-goddess has 'decline[d] her beams
as discontented' (l. 251), with the result that

> All droops, all dies, all trodden under dust
> The person, place, and passages forgotten,
> The hardest steel eaten with softest rust,
> The firm and solid tree both rent and rotten.

(ll. 253–6)

Elizabeth's personal mutability, identified with her femaleness, is seen as generating universal mutability and decay. It
is unlikely that Shakespeare knew Ralegh's poem, which

was not published or circulated, but, assuming that *The Ocean to Cynthia* does indeed belong to Ralegh's disgrace of 1592, it seems that both poem and play participate in a distinctive 1590s sense that the time is out of joint, and that this is attributable to the unbalanced exercise of female power.

In *A Midsummer Night's Dream*, the subjugation to male rulers and spouses of both the Amazon Queen Hippolyta and the Fairy Queen Titania is shown as a more natural state of affairs than unbridled female autonomy. Both figures could be associated with Elizabeth I, but in ways which were tangential and necessarily evasive of direct negative implications. Elizabeth was frequently represented as a warrior-woman, especially in the wake of the Armada victory of 1588. However, images of her specifically as an Amazon were comparatively rare. . . .

CURTAILING FEMALE POWER

I do not want to suggest, then, that Hippolyta or Titania are direct one-for-one representations of Elizabeth. Indeed, on the face of it, Elizabeth and Titania could not be more different. Elizabeth as imperial votaress is shown as ethereally impregnable to desire, whereas Titania is dominated by desire, first wilfully, in her attachment to the Indian prince, then humiliatingly and punitively, in her subjection to desire for an ass. In fact, Elizabeth is specifically exempted from sexuality by its displacement on to Titania: it is because the imperial votaress glides away immune to Cupid's arrow that it falls on the flower which enables Titania's enslavement to passion for Bottom. The penalties inflicted by the Elizabethan state for publications which incurred official displeasure could be brutal—in 1579, for instance, John Stubbs and William Page each had his right hand cut off for respectively writing and distributing a pamphlet opposing Elizabeth's current marriage negotiations. Northrop Frye points to this as evidence that Titania could not possibly be a reference to Elizabeth: 'The consequences to Shakespeare's dramatic career if the Queen had believed that she was being publicly represented as having a love affair with a jackass are something we fortunately don't have to think about.' However, such literal-mindedness seems inappropriate; instead, I would suggest that Patterson's idea of functional ambiguity is useful here. It is precisely because he has carefully distinguished Titania, and Hippolyta, from

Elizabeth that Shakespeare is able to use them to explore the desirability of curtailing female power, an exploration which can itself, in safely indirect and encoded form, express the prevalent sense of unease with Elizabeth's female authority.

Noel Purdon points out that Titania's degradation belongs to an ancient mythological tradition of the goddess or queen who is punished or diminished by being made to fall in love with a mortal or animal. Examples of this include Venus with Adonis, Pasiphae, mother of the Minotaur, with a bull; and Selene, a Greek name for the moon-goddess, with Endymion, a shepherd. *A Midsummer Night's Dream* is a play in which, emphatically, women are brought into line, and authority rests in the hands of fathers and husbands, dukes and kings. Even when Hermia and Helena finally get the husbands of their choice, it is not through their own powers but through the overruling of Hermia's father by an even higher patriarchal figure, Theseus —for whom the multiple wedding affirms his own conjugal possession of Hippolyta—and through the aid of another patriarchal figure, the Fairy King.

This is one of the many Shakespeare plays in which mothers, figures of female power within the familial structure, are curiously absent. Only two mothers are mentioned, and even then only to be marginalized and excluded: the mother of the changeling boy, Titania's Indian votaress, is dead, her life sacrificed for her boy-child (II. i. 135); Thisbe's mother is the part originally assigned to Starveling (I. ii. 53), but she is silently deleted and in Act V he appears instead as the Man in the Moon. Theseus's lecture to Hermia on filial disobedience in Act I figures conception itself as the quasi-divine act of a male progenitor alone, justifying absolute paternal authority:

> To you your father should be as a god,
> One that composed your beauties, yea, and one
> To whom you are but as a form in wax,
> By him imprinted, and within his power
> To leave the figure or disfigure it.

(I. i. 47–51)

Set against this view, though, and despite being safely placed in the past of the play, Titania's Indian votaress is a memorable figure of female fertility who inspires one of the richest passages in the text which cannot be easily ignored or forgotten. Titania tells how:

> Full often hath she gossiped by my side,
> And sat with me on Neptune's yellow sands,
> Marking th'embarkèd traders on the flood,

When we have laughed to see the sails conceive
And grow big-bellied with the wanton wind,
Which she with pretty and with swimming gait
Following, her womb then rich with my young squire,
Would imitate, and sail upon the land
To fetch me trifles, and return again
As from a voyage, rich with merchandise.

(II. i. 125–34)

The two women together mocked the 'big-bellied' sails of merchant ships as mere travesties of pregnancy, the votaress triumphantly flaunting the fruitfulness of her own womb. For G. Wilson Knight, this scene represents fairyland deriding the worldly preoccupations of humanity: 'as we watch Titania and her loved friend laughing at the "traders on the flood", imitating their "voyage" on the waters of life, we see fairyland laughing at storm-tossed mortality.' While the observation is valuable, I think we can go further to acknowledge the significance of gender here: Titania and the votaress are emphatically female, and the merchant ships are the vehicles of men's exploits and ventures. From the female viewpoint of the shore, the ships are inconsequential, their cargoes no more than 'trifles' equivalent to pretty flotsam (l. 133), their sails hollow, filled only with wind.

The most serious challenge to male authority in the play, the only truly equivalent force, is the uncontained fertile female sexuality represented by the Indian votaress, by Titania's league with her and intense maternal affection for her son, and then by Titania's passion for Bottom, which seems to take Oberon by surprise in its consuming intensity (IV. i. 45–60). At the same time Titania's voluptuously and magnificently pregnant votaress is a telling contrast to the chaste, watery, ethereal, imperial votaress described by Oberon in his account of his vision. The opposition highlights the fact that, although the imperial votaress is ostensibly revered for her chastity, this is at odds with the values of the rest of *A Midsummer Night's Dream*. Her perpetual and impregnable virginity renders her not only exceptional, mystical and quasi-divine, but also ghostly and almost deathly as she floats untouched across the scene, and she is identified with a moon which is chilly, insipid and dampening (II. i. 162). By contrast, the Indian votaress sails upon the land, and has a corresponding generous materiality expressed in language not only of richness, abundance, and fullness, but also of merriment and pleasure.

The overall attitude of the play to perpetual virginity is also plainly expressed in the diction of enclosure and sterility in Theseus's lines to Hermia: as a nun she would be a 'barren sister', 'in shady cloister mewed', chanting hymns which were 'faint' to a moon which was 'cold' and 'fruitless' (I. i. 71–3). Rather than the static agelessness and timelessness of the imperial votaress, it is the 'quick bright things' of love and youth that the play invites its audience to enjoy (I. i. 149). Self-willed female desire is the most serious threat to the patriarchal order in the play and the source of its struggle and conflict; correspondingly, though, the happy outcome of the struggle, the 'concord of this discord' (V. i. 60), is the realignment of female sexuality with patriarchy, not its denial. The play prizes female sexuality which is directed into marriage and motherhood far more highly than sterile purity, and identifies it with the central values of fruitfulness, warmth and harmony as the four couples—not only the three Athenian pairs but also Oberon and Titania—move towards their final marital unions.

The direct reference to Elizabeth in the 'imperial vot'ress' passage has been read by some scholars as a compliment designed to be given in her presence in the play's audience. Linked with the *Dream*'s prominent nuptial theme, this has inspired further speculation that the play was originally composed as part of the celebrations of an aristocratic wedding which the Queen attended. However, in the contexts of both the ambivalent moon-imagery of the 1590s, and the attitude of the play as a whole towards absolute virginity, it becomes difficult to read the 'imperial vot'ress' passage as an unequivocal compliment to the Queen. As Louis Montrose puts it, the action of the play 'depends upon her absence, her exclusion.' On other grounds of theatrical history and the nature of the play, some distinguished editors have provided strong arguments against the theory of performance at a royally attended aristocratic wedding. Whether delivered in Elizabeth's presence or not, though, both the 'imperial vot'ress' passage and the whole play could have served as a functionally ambiguous critique, whose negative implications were detectable but sufficiently veiled to evade open provocation. The principal interest of the play is not in iconic virginity, but in the progress and processes of love.

May Games and Metamorphoses

C.L. Barber

C.L. Barber's influential study *Shakespeare's Festive Comedy* explores the fantastic element of *A Midsummer Night's Dream.* Barber, formerly professor of English at Amherst College, stresses the liberating and transforming power of the festive spirit that infuses the play. He suggests that the fairies are "embodiments of the May-game experience of eros," and that the young lovers are subjugated by the power of love, which is more a force of nature than a construct of civilization.

If Shakespeare had called *A Midsummer Night's Dream* by a title that referred to pageantry and May games, the aspects of it with which I shall be chiefly concerned would be more often discussed. To honor a noble wedding, Shakespeare gathered up in a play the sort of pageantry which was usually presented piece-meal at aristocratic entertainments, in park and court as well as in hall. And the May game, everybody's pastime, gave the pattern for his whole action, which moves "from the town to the grove" and back again, bringing in summer to the bridal. These things were familiar and did not need to be stressed by a title.

Shakespeare's young men and maids, like those [Phillip] Stubbes described in May games, "run gadding over night to the woods, ... where they spend the whole night in pleasant pastimes—" and in the fierce vexation which often goes with the pastimes of falling in and out of love and threatening to fight about it. "And no marvel," Stubbes exclaimed about such headlong business, "for there is a great Lord present among them, as superintendent and Lord over their pastimes and sports, namely, Satan, prince of hell." In making Oberon, prince of fairies, into the May king, Shakespeare urbanely plays with the notion of a supernatural power at work in holiday: he presents the common May game presided over by an aristocratic garden god. Titania is a Summer Lady who "waxeth wounder proud":

> I am a spirit of no common rate,
> The summer still doth tend upon my state . . .
>
> (III.i.157–158)

And Puck, as jester, promotes the "night-rule" version of misrule over which Oberon is superintendent and lord in the "haunted grove." The lovers originally meet

> in the wood, a league without the town,
> Where I did meet thee once with Helena
> To do observance to a morn of May.
>
> (I.i.165–167)

Next morning, when Theseus and Hippolyta find the lovers sleeping, it is after their own early "observation is performed" —presumably some May-game observance, of a suitably aristocratic kind, for Theseus jumps to the conclusion that

> No doubt they rose up early to observe
> The rite of May; and, hearing our intent,
> Came here in grace of our solemnity.
>
> (IV.i.135–137)

These lines need not mean that the play's action happens on May Day. Shakespeare does not make himself accountable for exact chronological inferences; the moon that will be new according to Hippolyta will shine according to Bottom's almanac. And in any case, people went Maying at various times, "Against May, Whitsunday, and other time" is the way Stubbes puts it. This Maying can be thought of as happening on a midsummer night, even on Midsummer Eve itself, so that its accidents are complicated by the delusions of a magic time. (May Week at Cambridge University still comes in June.) The point of the allusions is not the date, but the *kind* of holiday occasion. The Maying is completed when Oberon and Titania with their trains come into the great chamber to bring the blessings of fertility. They are at once common and special, a May king and queen making their good luck visit to the manor house, and a pair of country gods, half-English and half-Ovid, come to bring their powers in tribute to great lords and ladies.

PAGEANTRY AND THE QUEEN

The play's relationship to pageantry is most prominent in the scene where the fairies are introduced by our seeing their quarrel. This encounter is the sort of thing that [Queen] Elizabeth and the wedding party might have happened on while walking about in the park during the long summer dusk. The fairy couple accuse each other of the usual weakness of pageant personages—a compelling love for royal personages:

> Why art thou here,
> Come from the farthest steep of India,
> But that, forsooth, the bouncing Amazon,
> Your buskin'd mistress and your warrior love,
> To Theseus must be wedded, and you come
> To give their bed joy and prosperity?
>
> (II.i.68–73)

Oberon describes an earlier entertainment, very likely one in which the family of the real-life bride or groom had been concerned:

> My gentle Puck, come hither. Thou rememb'rest
> Since once I sat upon a promontory
> And heard a mermaid, on a dolphin's back . . .
> That very time I saw (but thou couldst not)
> Flying between the cold moon and the earth
> Cupid, all arm'd. A certain aim he took
> At a fair Vestal, throned by the West,
> And loos'd his love-shaft smartly from his bow,
> As it should pierce a hundred thousand hearts.
> But I might see young Cupid's fiery shaft
> Quench'd in the chaste beams of the wat'ry moon,
> And the imperial vot'ress passed on,
> In maiden meditation, fancy-free.
>
> (II.i.147–164)

At the entertainment at Elvetham in 1591, Elizabeth was throned by the west side of a garden lake to listen to music from the water; the fairy queen came with a round of dancers and spoke of herself as wife to Auberon. These and other similarities make it quite possible, but not necessary, that Shakespeare was referring to the Elvetham occasion. . . .

OVID AND METAMORPHOSES

As we have seen, it was commonplace to imitate Ovid. Ovidian fancies pervade *A Midsummer Night's Dream*, and especially the scene of the fairy quarrel: the description of the way Cupid "loos'd his love shaft" at Elizabeth parallels the *Metamorphoses'* account of the god's shooting "his best arrow, with the golden head" at Apollo; Helena, later in the scene, exclaims that "The story shall be chang'd:/ Apollo flies, and Daphne holds the chase"—and proceeds to invert animal images from Ovid. The game was not so much to lift things gracefully from Ovid as it was to make up fresh things in Ovid's manner, as Shakespeare here, by playful mythopoesis, explains the bad weather by his fairies' quarrel and makes up a metamorphosis of the little Western flower to motivate the play's follies and place Elizabeth superbly above them. The pervasive Ovidian influence accounts for Theseus' putting fables and fairies in the same breath when he says, punning on ancient and antic,

> I never may believe
> These antique fables nor these fairy toys.
>
> (V.i.2–3)

The humor of the play relates superstition, magic and passionate delusion as "fancy's images." The actual title emphasizes a sceptical attitude by calling the comedy a "dream." It seems unlikely that the title's characterization of the dream, "a midsummer night's dream," implies association with the specific customs of Midsummer Eve, the shortest night of the year, except as "midsummer night" would carry suggestions of a magic time. . . . Shakespeare's imagination found its way to similarities with folk cult, starting from the custom of Maying and the general feeling that spirits may be abroad in the long dusks and short nights of midsummer. Olivia in *Twelfth Night* speaks of "midsummer madness" (III.iv.61). In the absence of evidence, there is no way to settle just how much comes from tradition. But what is clear *is* that Shakespeare was not *simply* writing out folklore which he heard in his youth, as Romantic critics liked to assume. On the contrary, his fairies are produced by a complex fusion of pageantry and popular game, as well as popular fancy. Moreover, as we shall see, they are not serious in the menacing way in which the people's fairies were serious. Instead they are serious in a very different way, as embodiments of the May-game experience of eros in men and women and trees and flowers, while any superstitious tendency to believe in their literal reality is mocked. The whole night's action is presented as a release of shaping fantasy which brings clarification about the tricks of strong imagination. We watch a dream; but we are awake, thanks to pervasive humor about the tendency to take fantasy literally, whether in love, in superstition, or in Bottom's mechanical dramatics. . . .

FESTIVE TRANSFORMATIONS

We see the fairies meet by moonlight in the woods before we see the lovers arrive there, and so are prepared to see the mortals lose themselves. In *The Winter's Tale*, Perdita describes explicitly the transforming and liberating powers of the spring festival which in *A Midsummer Night's Dream* are embodied in the nightwood world the lovers enter. After Perdita has described the spring flowers, she concludes with

> O, these I lack
> To make you garlands of; and my sweet friend,
> To strew him o'er and o'er!
> FLORIZEL.   What, like a corse?
> PERDITA. No, like a bank for love to lie and play on;
> Not like a corse; or if—not to be buried,
> But quick, and in mine arms. Come, take your flow'rs.
> Methinks I play as I have seen them do
> In Whitsun pastorals. Sure this robe of mine
> Does change my disposition.
>
> (*WT* IV.iv.127–135)

Her recovery is as exquisite as her impulse towards surrender: she comes back to herself by seeing her gesture as the expression of the occasion. . . .

The lovers in *A Midsummer Night's Dream* play "as in Whitsun pastorals," but they are entirely without this sort of consciousness of their folly. They are unreservedly *in* the passionate protestations which they rhyme at each other as they change partners:

> HELENA. Lysander, if you live, good sir, awake.
> LYSANDER. And run through fire I will for thy sweet sake
> Transparent Helena!
>
> (II.ii.102–104)

The result of this lack of consciousness is that they are often rather dull and undignified, since however energetically they elaborate conceits, there is usually no qualifying irony, nothing withheld. And only accidental differences can be exhibited, Helena tall, Hermia short. Although the men think that "reason says" now Hermia, now Helena, is "the worthier maid," personalities have nothing to do with the case: it is the flowers that bloom in the spring. The life in the lovers' parts is not to be caught in individual speeches, but by regarding the whole movement of the farce, which swings and spins each in turn through a common pattern, an evolution that seems to have an impersonal power of its own. . . .

LOVE AS AN IMPERSONAL FORCE

The farce is funniest, and most meaningful, in the climactic scene where the lovers are most unwilling, where they try their hardest to use personality to break free, and still are willy-nilly swept along to end in pitch darkness, trying to fight. When both men have arrived at wooing Helena, she assumes it must be voluntary mockery, a "false sport" fashioned "in spite." She appeals to Hermia on the basis of their relation as particular individuals, their "sister's vows." But Hermia is at sea, too; names no longer work: "Am I not Hermia? Are not you Lysander?" So in the end Hermia too, though she has held off, is swept into the whirl, attacking Helena as a thief of love. She grasps at straws to explain what has happened by something manageably related to their individual identities:

> HELENA. Fie, fie! You counterfeit, you puppet you.
> HERMIA. Puppet? Why so! Ay, that way goes the game.
> Now I perceive that she hath made compare
> Between our statures; she hath urg'd her height . . .
> How low am I, thou painted maypole? Speak!
>
> (III.ii.289–296)

In exhibiting a more drastic helplessness of will and mind than anyone experienced in *Love's Labour's Lost*, this farce conveys a sense of people being tossed about by a force which puts them beside themselves to take them beyond themselves. The change that happens is presented simply, with little suggestion that it involves a growth in insight—Demetrius is not led to realize something false in his diverted affection for Hermia. But one psychological change, fundamental in growing up, is presented. Helena tries at first to move Hermia by an appeal to "schooldays friendship, childhood innocence," described at length in lovely, generous lines:

> So we grew together,
> Like to a double cherry, seeming parted,
> But yet an union in partition—
> Two lovely berries molded on one stem . . .
> And will you rent our ancient love asunder
> To join with men in scorning your poor friend?
>
> (III.ii.208–216)

"To join with men" has a plaintive girlishness about it. But before the scramble is over, the two girls have broken the double-cherry bond, to fight each without reserve for her man. So they move from the loyalties of one stage of life to those of another. When it has happened, when they wake up, the changes in affections seem mysterious. So Demetrius says

> But, my good lord, I wot not by what power
> (But by some power it is) my love to Hermia,
> Melted as the snow, seems to me now

As the remembrance of an idle gaud
Which in my childhood I did dote upon . . .

                                        (IV.i.167–171)

The comedy's irony about love's motives and choices expresses love's power not as an attribute of special personality but as an impersonal force beyond the persons concerned. . . .

Shakespeare, in developing a May-game action at length
to express the will in nature that is consummated in marriage, brings out underlying magical meanings of the ritual
while keeping always a sense of what it is humanly, as an
experience. The way nature is felt is shaped . . . by the things
that are done in encountering it. The woods are a region of
passionate excitement where, as Berowne said, love "adds a
precious seeing to the eye." This precious seeing was talked
about but never realized in *Love's Labour's Lost;* instead we
got wit. But now it is realized; we get poetry. Poetry conveys
the experience of amorous tendency diffused in nature; and
poetry, dance, gesture, dramatic fiction, combine to create,
in the fairies, creatures who embody the passionate mind's
elated sense of its own omnipotence. The woods are established as a region of metamorphosis, where in liquid moonlight or glimmering starlight, things can change, merge and
melt into each other. Metamorphosis expresses both what
love sees and what it seeks to do.

Literary Influences on *A Midsummer Night's Dream*

R.A. Foakes

A Midsummer Night's Dream is one of Shakespeare's most original plays in that its main plot is not derived from another story. Yet the play is heavily indebted to a wide range of literary and folkloric sources, as is evident in the following essay by R.A. Foakes, an editor of the play and professor of English at the University of California, Los Angeles. Shakespeare makes substantial use of plays by John Lyly, stories by Chaucer and Ovid, as well as characters from French romance and English folklore, blending these diverse strands into a unique and satisfying work of art.

The word 'source' is clumsy in relation to a play like *A Midsummer Night's Dream*. Shakespeare used or adapted names, ideas, images or hints for incidents from various works he certainly knew, and echoed a number more, so that a long list of works can be compiled that probably contributed in some way to the play. The detection of these has its own fascination and is useful in so far as they illustrate the workings of Shakespeare's imagination, but the most notable feature of the play is the dramatist's inventiveness, brilliantly fusing scattered elements from legend, folklore and earlier books and plays into a whole that remains as fresh and original now as when it was composed. The range of reference underlying it deserves attention also, however, because it helps to explain something of the archetypal force of the comedy, showing the dramatist's instinct for seizing on whatever might articulate and enrich the web of meanings and relationships developed in it.

A play so much concerned with transformation transforms its sources, none more so than the work which has recently been proposed as 'the primary influence' on it, and indeed a major source for it, namely John Lyly's *Gallathea* (? 1585; printed 1592). Shakespeare certainly knew the plays of Lyly, and in *A Midsummer Night's Dream* he built up the action 'in the manner of Lyly, by balancing a number of self-contained groups, one against the other', and presenting each group in turn. In drawing attention to Lyly's influence in this general way, G.K. Hunter pointed especially to *Sapho and Phao* (not published until 1632) and *Midas* (1589; printed 1592), in which Midas's head is 'metamorphosed' (4.1.168) into an ass's head, anticipating Bottom's transformation. In her more recent essay, Leah Scragg claims that *Gallathea* was much more directly influential on Shakespeare's play in its concern with love in relation to 'a pervasive process of metamorphosis'. . . . Whatever hints Shakespeare picked up from Lyly he developed beyond recognition, so that the differences are far more remarkable than the similarities, and G.K. Hunter's account of Lyly's impact on Shakespeare remains persuasive; he assessed Lyly's dramatic achievement sympathetically, and showed too how Shakespeare went beyond him in *A Midsummer Night's Dream* to create 'a whole realm of action whose poetic atmosphere is alone sufficient to characterize the ideas it contains'.

The framing device of the play—the wedding celebrations of Theseus—Shakespeare developed from the narrative in Chaucer's *The Knight's Tale*, which refers to the conquest by Theseus of the Amazons and their queen, Hippolyta (1. 866–83), and the great 'solempnytee' and feast of the wedding (compare 'the night / Of our solemnities', 1.1.10–11). In Chaucer's poem Theseus is represented as a keen hunter, riding out 'With hunte and horn and houndes him bisyde' (1. 1678; compare 4.1.100 ff.). Chaucer stresses the wisdom, dignity and great state of Theseus, and Shakespeare clouded his picture by taking from Sir Thomas North's translation of Plutarch's 'Life of Theseus' the names of various women he was there said to have loved and abandoned (2.1.77–80). Shakespeare's Theseus, if Oberon (and Plutarch) can be believed, had doted like the lovers in the play, whose story also owes something to Chaucer. In *The Knight's Tale* Theseus returns home to Athens after his wedding to be stopped by a 'compaignye of ladyes'(1, 898) kneeling in the highway and seeking his help against the 'tiraunt Creon'(1, 961) of Thebes, who has refused to allow them to bury their husbands, killed in battle. Theseus in turn slays Creon, and in the fight takes prisoner two young knights, friends and cousins, Palamon and Arcite, who both fall in love with Emily when, from their prison tower, they see her setting out to 'do May observance' (1, 1047, 1500; compare 1.1.167). Their story, involving their meeting in a wood after Arcite's release and Palamon's escape, and their quarrel arising from a clash between love and friendship, suggested the escape of the lovers to a wood in *A Midsummer Night's Dream*, as well as their quarrels and eventual reconciliation. Shakespeare, of course, creates two pairs of lovers and transfers the emphasis on friendship and 'sisters' vows' (3.2.199) to the girls, Hermia and Helena. In Chaucer's tale, Theseus, out hunting on a May morning, comes upon Palamon and Arcite fighting one another for the love of Emily; in the play, Theseus, again out hunting, encounters the two pairs of lovers asleep in 4.1, supposing they have risen 'early to observe / The rite of May' (4.1.129–30). Shakespeare also borrowed the names Philostrate and Egeus from Chaucer; Philostrate is the alias adopted by Arcite at 1, 1428, and Egeus is the name of the old father of Theseus (1, 2838, 2905). Shakespeare transformed the company of ladies who complain to Theseus at the beginning of *The Knight's Tale* into Egeus complaining against Hermia in 1.1.

THE FAIRY WORLD

Shakespeare probably derived the general idea for a King and Queen of Fairies who quarrel between themselves, and intervene in the affairs of human beings, from Chaucer's *Merchant's Tale*. Chaucer's king and queen are called Pluto and Proserpine, and the outcome of their debate about love, sex and the relations of wife and husband, in which Pluto attacks and Proserpine defends the treacheries of women, is that Pluto restores the sight of the old man January in time for him to see his wife, May, making love to the young squire Damian in a pear tree, while Proserpine ensures that May has the wit to persuade January to believe he imagined what he saw. Like Pluto and Proserpine, Oberon and Titania take sides in their support respectively for Hippolyta and Theseus, but Shakespeare richly develops the basic idea by making his fairy king a lover of Hippolyta, and Titania a lover of Theseus, by inventing their quarrel over the Indian boy, and by providing them with a train of fairies and adding Puck; although in Chaucer's tale Pluto is King of the Fairies, no fairies appear, and he is somewhat oddly accompanied by 'many a lady' (IV, 2228).

The name Oberon derives from the romance *Huon of Bordeaux*, translated by Lord Berners (first published 1533–42), and well enough known to have provided matter for a play, no longer extant, in the repertory of the Earl of Sussex's Men in 1593–4, and for incidents in Robert Greene's play *The Scottish History of James IV* (?1590), which turns history into romance, and gives Oberon a marginal role at the opening and later on when he brings on fairies dancing in rounds. In *Huon of Bordeaux* Oberon and his fairies are associated with the east; they inhabit a wood, they can create illusory storms and dangers, all 'fantasie and enchauntments', and they can make mortals think they are in paradise. When Huon encounters them he is on his way to Babylon to see a maid, 'the most fairest creature in all *Inde*', and this may have suggested to Shakespeare the association of Oberon and Titania with India (2.1.69,124). The name Titania is a patronymic used several times by Ovid in the *Metamorphoses* in reference to descendants of the Titans, such as Pyrrha, Latona, Diana and Circe. Shakespeare apparently borrowed the name from the Latin, since Arthur Golding never uses it in his translation of the *Metamorphoses* (1567, reprinted for the fourth time in 1593), which the dramatist knew well, and which provided him with a version of the Pyramus and Thisbe story.

If Oberon comes from romance, and Titania from classical legend, Puck seems to have originated as a generic name in Old English for mischievous, or sometimes malicious, spirits, and came to be used in the sixteenth century as a specific name for a 'shrewd and knavish sprite' (2.1.33) also known as Hobgoblin and Robin Goodfellow. Many of Puck's attributes in *A Midsummer Night's Dream* were traditional—his mocking laughter 'Ho, ho, ho', (3.2.421), his broom to sweep 'behind the door', so helping housemaids who left milk for him (5.1.367–8), and his ability to take on any shape (2.1.46–55). Shakespeare makes him merry and impish, a practical joker acting more in fun than malice, and so perhaps established a popular image of Puck, who is elsewhere sometimes depicted as devilish, as in *Wily Beguiled* (1602). Puck or Robin Goodfellow was a familiar figure in Shakespeare's day, in legend, ballad and drama, and he appears with his broom in Jonson's masque *Love Restored* (1616). Bullough and most editors take it for granted that Shakespeare picked up hints for his Puck from Reginald Scot's *Discoverie of Witchcraft* (1584); certainly Scot summarises the traditional characteristics of Robin, though I doubt whether Shakespeare needed to consult him to learn what was common knowledge. Scot interestingly records that belief in such spirits was passing away: 'heretofore Robin Goodfellow, and Hobgoblin were as terrible, and also as credible to the people, as hags and witches be now: and in time to come, a witch will be as much derided and contemned and as plainlie perceived, as the illusion and knaverie of Robin Goodfellow'. Shakespeare gave him immortality by transforming him into his 'merry wanderer of the night' (2.1.43).

Puck was probably played by an adult actor, as in *Grim the Collier of Croydon* (1600), where he appears as the clownish servant of the devil, for he is called a 'lob' or bumpkin by a fairy at 2.1.16. The fairies in the play are, by contrast, imagined as tiny, and Shakespeare teases the imagination of his audience by requiring them to accept that his actors were as diminutive as their names Cobweb and Mustardseed suggest. . . .

Fairies might be malevolent, as is made clear in *Cymbeline,* where Imogen prays for protection from 'fairies and the tempters of the night' (2.2.9), and in *Hamlet,* where Marcellus says that at Christmas 'No fairy takes, nor witch hath power to harm' (1.1.163). Oberon explicitly distinguishes the fairies in A *Midsummer Night's Dream* from witches and tempters of the night: 'we are spirits of another sort' (3.2.388). Shakespeare's fairies belong, like those in *The Merry Wives of Windsor* 5.5, to an equally strong tradition of more kindly fairies, who may pinch sluttish housemaids, but reward those who do well and say their prayers, and bring them good fortune, as in Greene's *James IV,* where Oberon's interventions are all benevolent, or in Lyly's *Endymion,* in which fairies, as the servants of Cynthia (or Diana, the moon), pinch Corsitas for his 'trespass' against her and afflict him with spots, but kiss the hero Endymion. In *Huon of Bordeaux,* Oberon says he 'was never devyll nor yll creature', and the image of fairies as well-disposed to the good was encouraged by Spenser's *Faerie Queene,* in which Oberon becomes a quasi-sacred figure as father of Gloriana, who allegorically represented Queen Elizabeth. The traditional sense of fairies as 'friendly' to human beings, or at least as rewarding the good and punishing the idle or bad, is, however, modified by Shakespeare in *A Midsummer Night's Dream,* in which he transforms his fairies on the one hand into Oberon and Titania, who have human passions and jealousies, and on the other hand into their train of delightfully innocuous figures, whose main office is tending their queen, protecting her from beetles, spiders and other night-creatures (2.2.9–23), and serving Bottom on her behalf as airy spirits (3.1.142 ff.). In envisaging them so, Shakespeare perhaps took a hint from the fairies with 'fair faces' who dance and sing in Lyly's *Endymion* 4.3 and dance and play in *Gallathea* 2.3, for in his company of boy-actors, it seems probable that the smallest and most nimble performed these parts. All the fairies join at the end in song and dance to bless the house of Theseus, so that the final image is of creatures who have power to ward off evil.

BOTTOM'S TRANSFORMATION

Shakespeare needed no other source than imagination working on life to create Bottom, Quince and the mechanicals—together with the presence in his company of the well-known clown Will Kemp and the slighter comedian Richard Cowley, a nicely matched pair who later created the parts of Dogberry and Verges. Bottom's transformation is a brilliant invention, linking him and his crew to the fairies and the lovers, and also to a range of well-known tales and legends of men changed into monsters. These go back to Circe in the *Odyssey,* and her power 'most monstrous shapes to frame' is also described in the *Metamorphoses,* translated by Arthur Golding (XIV, 63); there were, however, two famous stories of men changed to asses. One was the legend of the foolish King Midas, who refused to accept the general verdict that Apollo had beaten Pan in a musical contest, and was therefore punished by the god, who changed his ears into ass's ears, leaving the rest of his body human (Golding's *Metamorphoses* XI, 165–216). This story was dramatised by John Lyly in his *Midas* (1589; published 1592), in which Apollo inflicts 'The ears of an ass upon the head of a king' (4.1.149–50), until eventually when Midas repents his folly, as the stage direction at 5.3.121 puts it, 'The ears fall off.'

    The other well-known tale of the transformation of a man into an ass occurs in Apuleius, *The Golden Ass,* translated by William Adlington (1566; other editions in 1571, 1582 and 1596). In Book 3, ch. 17 Apuleius persuades his mistress Fotis, the servant of a witch, to steal a box of ointment and anoint him with it, in the expectation that he will be changed into a bird, only to find that he is completely transformed into an ass and, what is worse, treated as one by other asses and horses, and by the thieves who take him and use him as a beast of burden. Apuleius as an ass is made to serve the thieves, and later helps a young maid they have captured to escape; she promises to reward him: 'I will bravely dress the haires of thy forehead, and then will I finely combe thy maine, I will tye up thy rugged tayle trimly . . . I will bring thee daily in my apron the kirnels of nuts, and will pamper thee up with delicates' (Book 6, ch. 23). This may have given Shakespeare a hint for Titania's courtesies to Bottom. If these antecedents were not enough, Shakespeare could also have found in Reginald Scot's *Discoverie of Witchcraft* the story of a young English visitor being transformed into an ass by a witch in Cyprus (Book v, ch. iii), and a description of a charm to 'set an horsse or an asses head upon a mans shoulders' (Book xii, ch. xx).

THE INFLUENCE OF OVID

This is the most notable of many changes of shape and trans-formations in the play, and probably the most pervasive influence on it is that of Ovid's *Metamorphoses,* mainly as mediated through the translation of Arthur Golding (1567). Shakespeare may have known the Latin text, but he would in any case have found in Golding's Ovid the story of Cupid's gold and leaden ar-rows (1.1.170), the personification of Hiems as an old man (2.1.109); the story of Apollo and Daphne (2.1.231); the legend of Philomel (2.2.13); the story of the battle between Hercules and the Centaurs (5.1.45); the description of the death of Orpheus at the hands of the Bacchanals (5.1.48); and the tale of Cephalus and Procris (5.1.194), as well as other suggestions for images. Golding's Ovid was also the main source for the story of Pyra-mus and Thisbe, and it was this version on which Shakespeare based the narrative action of the play staged by the mechanicals. Not only the general alignment of the 'tedious brief scene' of Pyramus and Thisbe with the story as told in Golding confirms this as the source, but the correspondence of a number of details which are different in other versions, such as the mantle dropped by Thisbe (5.1.141); the 'crannied hole' (5.1.156); 'Ni-nus' tomb' (5.1.137); and the mulberry tree (5.1.147).

Shakespeare probably knew several versions of the story, beginning with Chaucer's *Legend of Good Women,* where it is treated seriously and with some delicacy as a moral tale about true love. Other treatments, including Golding's, fall into unintended absurdities, and offered matter for Shakespeare to use or parody. Golding pads out his unwieldy lines with a liberal use of the pleonastic 'did', which Quince's prologue picks up to comic effect.

> Did scare away, or rather did affright;
> And as she fled, her mantle she did fall,
> Which Lion vile with bloody mouth did stain . . .
>
> (5.1.140–2)

Shakespeare also exaggerated the courtesy the lovers found in Golding's wall by having Snout play the part. . . .

One further very specific debt to Golding's Ovid is to be found in Titania's speech on the disorder in nature caused by her quarrel with Oberon in 2.1.81–114, where Shakespeare combined images from the description of the seasons with suggestions from various accounts of Deucalion's flood, plagues and curses. Other minor but significant echoes contribute to the play; the title of Quince's play appears to be a parody of the printed title of Thomas Preston's *Cambyses* (1570) and Bottom's alliterative 'part to tear a cat in' burlesques a passage in John Studley's translation of Seneca's *Hercules Oetaeus* (1581). Bottom's account of his vision takes off from a passage in St Paul's Epistle to the Corinthians (4.1.205–7). Some material for the development of Theseus, his amorous adventures, and devotion to Hercules, was taken from Plutarch's 'Life of Theseus', as translated by Sir Thomas North (1579). . . . It is exciting to discover connections, to track Shakespeare as a snapper-up of unconsidered trifles, hoarding like a magpie what others did not value, and transmuting it, at opportune moments, into dramatic gold. At the same time it is important to ask continually whether Shakespeare needed to go to a source for what was common property, or could have been on tap as flowing from an unconscious or subconscious assimilation of what was, so to speak, in the air, the common materials of the culture and discourse of his age. Judged on these terms, the other sources that have been claimed for incidents or passages in *A Midsummer Night's Dream* are dubious; all the same, the texture of the play derives a large part of its richness and complexity from the many imaginative strands Shakespeare drew from legend, folklore, literature and drama, and wove inextricably together to our lasting delight.

CHAPTER 2

The Plot of *A Midsummer Night's Dream*

READINGS ON
A MIDSUMMER NIGHT'S DREAM

The Exposition of the Plot in Act One

Harold F. Brooks

According to Professor Harold F. Brooks, of the University of London, the unity and coherence of *A Midsummer Night's Dream* is not dependent primarily on traditional notions of plot. Rather unity is achieved through patterns of correspondences between characters and through recurring motifs and themes. These patterns are brilliantly set up in the play's exposition in the first two scenes; also established there are the ultimate goal of the play's action—the wedding of Theseus and Hippolyta—as well as the dominant theme of the play, the relationship between love and marriage.

That *A Midsummer Night's Dream* was designed to grace a wedding is a presumption as strong as it can be in default of the direct evidence which would make it certain. Grant the presumption, and it accounts for the inclusion and clarifies the relevance of everything in the play. Reject it, and there can still be no doubt that love in relation to marriage is the dramatist's subject. It is the theme stated, along with the goal—a wedding—of the dramatic action, in the opening speech. The 'nuptial hour' of Theseus and Hippolyta 'draws on apace'; yet the brief time of waiting 'lingers' Theseus' 'desires': he is an ardent lover, and in her reply Hippolyta reciprocates his love. At once there falls across the prospect of this love-match the shadow of Egeus' demand for the enforcement of a marriage contrary to love. The action has begun which from his entry keeps step with an exposition, lucid and economical, that introduces not only the situation and characters, but other features of the play as well. When Puck has departed to fetch the magic flower, and Oberon has declared what he means to do with it, the exposition is complete.

By then, we have been made acquainted with the situations of conflict in the fairy world and for the young lovers. The lovers' initial roles as true or false in love and friendship have been established, with Helena further characterized, and Puck, and so far as is needful Oberon, Titania, and Theseus characterized too. The chief agents in the development of the plot have been given due prominence: Oberon, whose eavesdropping leads him to extend the action he purposed in his own conflict with Titania and to intervene also in the lovers' conflict; and Puck, his jester and minister, known for practical joking and shape-shifting, to whom he delegates that intervention. Familiar with plebeian mortals, as we have been reminded he is, Puck, in turn, will eavesdrop on the artisans and interfere with their project. The agent of which he and Oberon make use, the flower Love-in-idleness, has been dignified by a legendary origin, a metamorphosis in Ovid's manner. The centrality of these agents in complicating and then unravelling the plot, and involving in it the fairies, the quartet of lovers, and the artisans, is one of the main means by which the play is unified. Another is the single occasion to which we have learned its four stories are moving: the ducal marriage. The fairies have come to Athens to give it blessing; the artisans are preparing their performance as a contribution to the accompanying revels which Philostrate was instructed to set on foot; and the wedding-day, finally, was the term fixed for Hermia to arrive at the decision expected to settle the outcome of the four lovers' story.

PARALLEL RULERS

As one anticipates in Shakespeare, yet another means to dramatic unity is the pattern of correspondences. A salient one in the exposition is between the Athenian and the fairy courts: the fairy ruler at strife with his consort, planning to end her rebellion; the Athenian recently at strife with his consort-to-be, but having now made conquest of her: the love between their fairy counterparts interrupted; their own about to be consummated. In Bottom, the artisan world has its uncrowned king, and he is cast for the part of a lover whose love never is to be consummated: as Quince tells him (and with him any in the audience who do not know the tale), Pyramus 'dies most gallant for love'.

Each set of characters plays its part under the auspices of the moon, the measure, in Theseus' and Hippolyta's opening speeches, of the interval of time which is the only remaining impediment to their union. It is the interval occupied by the action of the comedy, of which the moon in its various aspects may be regarded as the regent. Before the exposition ends, it has been given significant roles for the young lovers, the artisans, and the fairies, as well as the ducal pair. When Hippolyta compares the new crescent to a silver bow the image is not only characteristic of herself, the Amazon huntress, accoutred probably as such, and to appear in that guise in the dawn scene; it is a reminder that the moon-goddess is also Diana, the virgin huntress of the woods. Moonlit woodland is to be the scene for the weaving of the plot entanglements and the preparations for their untangling. The move from Athens to the wood is made at the final stage of the exposition, introducing the fairies in their domain; and the audience knows that the four lovers and the artisans are bound thither. The Duke (as yet) is not; but the artisans' rendezvous is associated with him: 'at the Duke's oak we meet' is Quince's directive. Even before the wood is reached, Shakespeare has begun, by poetic reference and poetic imagery, to evoke the beauty of his natural setting. Hermia's voice, says Helena, is

> More tuneable than lark to shepherd's ear,
> When wheat is green, when hawthorn buds appear.

The assignation for the elopement is at the spot where Lysander once foregathered with the two girls

> To do observance to a morn of May;

the spot, Hermia tells her friend, where they two

> Upon faint primrose beds were wont to lie.

IMAGINATION AND JUDGEMENT

The midsummer night's experiences in the wood are to be the 'Dream' of the play's title (unless the whole play is so). Hippolyta has prophesied that in the interim before 'the night of our solemnities', daytime will quickly steep itself in night, and night will 'dream away the time.' Apparent experience as perhaps dream, or as governed by imagination, is a theme which comes to share the central focus in the final phases of the play, from the awakenings of Act IV to the epilogue; but it has been present all through as a subtext to the main theme of love and marriage. Love-sight, true and false, a principal motif in that main theme, belongs to the wide-ranging subject of appearance and reality, seldom far from Shakespeare's thought; a subject which includes the genuine though not rational insights of imagination, and its irrational aberrations. The importance of these themes right from the beginning of the play is well brought out by Frank Kermode's account of their place in the opening scene. Lysander is accused of having stamped himself upon Hermia's imagination by the customary specious methods of counterfeit love. She maintains that her vision of him is true love-sight, no induced fantasy, but valid: why can her father not see him so?

> I would my father look'd but with my eyes.

'Rather,' her judge admonishes her,

> Rather your eyes must with his judgement look.

Love-sight, imaginative, impressionable, and deceivable, must yield to paternal judgement, supposedly rational. Lysander makes it plain that Egeus can have no rational grounds for preferring Demetrius as his son-in-law. Rational or not, however, the paternal choice carries authority, and Hermia is required to 'fit your fancies to your father's will'. Lysander has put his own claim (and hers) on its true foundation:

> I am belov'd of beauteous Hermia.

Accepting his plea, as they rightly will, the play's audience will be accepting the trustworthiness of Hermia's intuitive love-sight. Yet the eyes, traditional initiators of love, are liable to see false under its irrational power: a fact typified by the love-juice, whose compulsive effect is to

> make or man or woman madly dote
> Upon the next live creature that it sees.

Love, Helena generalizes, 'looks not with the eyes'—eyes which but for love would report the object as it really is—'but with the mind'—a mind which has not 'of any judgement taste'. So, she complains, Demetrius who once could see her as all Athens does, a woman no less attractive than Hermia, and at that time made love to her, now having 'look'd on Hermia's eyne' cannot or will not see 'what all but he do know', and is infatuated with her friend. She herself, she confesses, cannot discard her own infatuation and, unworthy as Demetrius now is, still adores his qualities.

Shakespeare's word for such infatuation is 'doting'. In *Romeo* and the *Dream*, it is applied especially (but not ex-

clusively) to love persisted in even when met with indifference or aversion. While Romeo sighed for Rosaline, Friar
Lawrence rebuked him 'for doting, not for loving'. As
Demetrius 'errs, doting on Hermia's eyes, / So I' says Helena;
to whom Lysander's adieu (prophetic of the sequel) has been

> As you on him, Demetrius dote on you.

Indeed, the first we heard of her (Lysander again the
speaker) was of how

> she, sweet lady, dotes,
> Devoutly dotes, dotes in idolatry

upon Demetrius. These dotings would nowadays be called
fixations; a term which may make clearer to us the first parallel with them in the fairy plot: the fixation Titania has developed on the Indian boy. That was originally, like Helena's
for Demetrius, a love entirely admirable: it merited all the
sympathy won for it by her story of the boy's mother. But
now she 'makes him all her joy', arousing Oberon's jealousy,
and disrupting the vital alliance between him, as her husband and consort, and herself: she no longer sees him as she
ought. Her aberration is maternal, not sexual: but its importance, as with the others, lies in the sphere of love and marriage. Until the play nears its end, the theme of love and
marriage holds without a rival the centre of attention: the
imaginative disorders in the vision of reality are contribu-
tory to it. The profoundest source of the play's unity is thematic: the dominance of that theme, firmly established in
the exposition.

This masterly exposition contains in embryo virtually the
whole play, including the principles of its structure. The design presents a sequence of woodland scenes developing and
resolving the dramatic conflicts, and framed within scenes
laid in Athens. As part of the exposition, the transition has
been made from Theseus and the Athenian polity to Oberon
and the realm of magic in the wood; the transition is
matched subsequently in reverse.

Dreams and the Play's Structure

Peter Holland

Peter Holland, editor of the current Oxford edition of
A Midsummer Night's Dream, describes the plot as
symmetrical, framed around the scene at the play's
center, the love-match between the Queen of Fairies
Titania and the very earthly weaver Bottom. The basic action moves from Athens to the deepest woods
and returns to the court at Athens. But the play con-
futes traditional plot expectations by resolving all the
complications of the romantic comedy, including the
confusion of the four lovers and the quarrel between
Oberon and Titania, by the end of Act Four. Just as
unexpected, according to Holland, is the central action of the play: a series of characters falling asleep
and waking up transformed.

A Midsummer Night's Dream has a neat and symmetrical
scenic form. Acts 1 and 5 take place in Athens, Acts 2 to 4 in
the wood. Immediately preceding the move to the wood
comes the casting scene for Quince, Bottom and company
(1.2); Bottom is reunited with the others immediately after
the wood scenes (4.2), before the full Athenian splendours of
the court in Act 5. Mark Rose describes this shape as 'a double frame around the central panel', emphasizing the central
moment of the play as the union of extremes, Titania and
Bottom, at the end of 3.1, the point at which modern productions almost always place the interval.

As Rose also shows, the whole play consists of only seven
scenes, fewer than any other Shakespeare play. Two scenes in
Athens, three in the wood and then two in Athens again adds
up to a structure of almost ostentatious simplicity, a form of
visible shapeliness and formal discipline. Such scenic restraint contains and controls the opulent movement of the dif-

ferent groups of characters as their worlds flow and blur and collide in the wood. It also intensifies the perception of the double frame, a feature intensified in modern production by the three sets the play has conventionally been given: the court for 1.1 and 5.1, Quince's house for 1.2 and 4.2, the wood for the central panel.

To some extent, the movement of the play from city to country and back again is tied to the play's interest in May Day and its associated festivities. It was in the wood that Lysander once met Hermia with Helena, 'To do observance to a morn of May' (1.1.167), just as Theseus will mockingly suggest that the presence of the four lovers in the wood is because 'No doubt they rose up early to observe / The rite of May' (4.1.131-2). As [C.L.] Barber saw, at the beginning of his outstanding analysis of the significance of popular festivity for the play, 'the May game, everybody's pastime, gave the pattern for his whole action'. Maying and its other games need not take place only at May Day, hence its appearance in a play explicitly linked in its title to Midsummer Eve. The best description of May games is the attack on them by Phillip Stubbes in *The Anatomy of Abuses* (1583):

> Against May, Whitsunday, or other time all the young men and maids, old men and wives, run gadding over night to the woods, groves, hills, and mountains, where they spend all the night in pleasant pastimes . . . I have heard it credibly reported (and that *viva voce*) by men of great gravity and reputation, that of forty, three-score, or a hundred maids going to the wood over night, there have scarcely the third part of them returned home again undefiled.

Others put the figures even higher: 'I have heard of ten maidens which went to fetch May, and nine of them came home with child'.

This rustic celebration of fertility combines neatly with the pleasures of sex in the woods that Hermia resists when Lysander proposes it (2.2.45-71). But its presence in the play is set against the notion of Midsummer itself, strongly associated with bonfires, watches, magic and carnival parades. Midsummer Eve, one of the oldest of all festivals in its celebration of the summer solstice, the turning point of the year, was particularly a time when spirits were abroad, when particular plants must be gathered and when one might see one's future true love in the fires or through other magic. Spenser's *Epithalamion* (1595) also suggests links between Midsummer and marriage. But Shakespeare makes the two festivals, Midsummer and May, into a blur, refusing to limit the associations of the two holidays in order to create 'a more elusive festival time'.

STRUCTURAL TENSION

Such blurring of two calendrical events is echoed in the problems of the formal shape. The play's abstract design with its symmetries and balances is in tension with two aspects of the dramatic action in Act 5, the movement necessary to balance Act 1 and the completion of the outermost frame. In effect, with the solution of the problems and obstacles to the marriages of the lovers, the action of *A Midsummer Night's Dream*, the action that conventionally marks the process of comedy towards marriage, is complete by 4.1.197. Titania has been reconciled with Oberon, the mortal lovers paired off. Indeed, at 4.1.183–4, Theseus speaks what in any other play would have sounded suspiciously like a final couplet: 'Away with us to Athens. Three and three, / We'll hold a feast in great solemnity.' As Anne Barton notes,

> This couplet has the authentic ring of a comedy conclusion. Only one expectation generated by the comedy remains unfulfilled: the presentation of the Pyramus and Thisby play before the Duke and his bride. Out of this single remaining bit of material, Shakespeare constructs a fifth act which seems, in effect, to take place beyond the normal plot-defined boundaries of comedy.

The exploration of art and artifice as reflection and revaluation that constitutes 'Pyramus and Thisbe', the exploration of the nature of theatre that constitutes the workers' performance of their play and the exploration of social assimilation that constitutes the reactions of the male members of the on-stage audience, have no place in the conventional structures of comedy. In many ways, as my discussion of 'Pyramus and Thisbe' as jig has already suggested, Act 5 is formally extraneous to the action of the drama, however essential it may be to the formal shaping of the structure.

This tension between dramatic action and abstract form reaches its culmination in *A Midsummer Night's Dream* late in Act 5, for neither the formal shape nor the dramatic action prescribes that anything should follow the exit of the aristocrats. Again Theseus 'is given a couplet which sounds like the last lines of a play' (5.1.360–1); again the play proves not to have ended. The arrival of Robin and then the rest of the

fairies, another opportunity in nineteenth-century productions for grand transformations and spectacle, must be unexpected. Just as, when Pyramus is dead, Bottom leaps up, res-
urrected, to offer an epilogue or a dance (5.1.345–6), so the
play will offer both an epilogue and the spectacle of the fairies
dancing and singing. For once 'Pyramus and Thisbe' proves
predictive as well as retrospective in its relation to *A Midsummer Night's Dream.*

Wherever Robin comes from, the audience cannot have assumed that he would enter the world of the palace, move from
wood to court, from country to city. Even though from the first
the presence of the fairies near Athens has been caused by the
royal wedding, with Oberon 'Come from the farthest step of
India, / . . . To give their bed joy and prosperity' (2.1.69, 73),
even though Oberon has announced that they 'will tomorrow
midnight solemnly / Dance in Duke Theseus' house, triumphantly' (4.1.87–8), the play's form had seemed to trap
them in the forest, just as Robin has assumed that they are
trapped by the hours of night (3.2.378–87). The final arrival of
the fairies, as the mortals go off to make love and to sleep, is
the audience's privilege: even more than Bottom, the audience is granted a 'most rare vision'.

SLEEP AND DREAMS

This structural peculiarity, this deliberate transformation of
dramatic form and expectation is one of the great glories of
the play. But the play has also posed dramatic difficulties in its
central sequence in the wood. No other Shakespeare play creates the potential awkwardness of leaving members of the
cast inconveniently around on stage in such profusion, im-
mobile because asleep. From the moment of Titania's falling
asleep at 2.2.30 to Bottom's awaking in 4.1, the problem is frequently repeated. Titania stays asleep till 3.1.122, over 250
lines of text. Hermia and Lysander sleep from 2.2.71 to 109
(Lysander) and 151 (Hermia). Demetrius sleeps from 3.2.87 to
137. All four of the lovers start to fall asleep from 3.2.420, stay-
ing asleep till 4.1.137 (over 170 lines). Titania and Bottom fall
asleep at 4.1.44; she wakes up at 4.1.75, he sleeps on till
4.1.198. At one point six different characters are asleep on
stage at once, presumably in two distinct groupings. No wonder that nineteenth-century productions, as they displayed
various parts of the wood, often let the lovers disappear from
sight, bringing them back on, . . . only when the mists clear. . . .

In a play about dream we should not be surprised that the stage shows us sleepers. But *A Midsummer Night's Dream* also makes of sleep the mark of a series of crucial transitions in the play. Titania asleep is drugged and will wake to fall in love with Bottom, Lysander and Demetrius undergo similar transformations as they sleep. Hermia wakes, having dreamed, to find Lysander gone. Titania wakes again to find 'My Oberon' (4.1.75); the four lovers will wake from sleep into that wonderfully ambivalent state of half-waking half-dreaming that they describe so wonderingly in 4.1; Bottom wakes to try, like them, to recall his dream.

The 'visions' Titania had in which 'I was enamoured of an ass' (4.1.75–6) can be changed, by being proved no dream, into something loathsome: 'O, how mine eyes do loathe his visage now' (l. 78). The mortals' experience, once they have recounted their dreams 'by the way' (l. 197) both to each other and to Theseus and Hippolyta, is much more complex, for they will never be able to see that their visions were no

---

SLEEPING ON STAGE

A Midsummer Night's Dream *is a very radical play in that the central action involves falling asleep, dreaming, and waking up. As Michael Mangan observes, this process is ultimately therapeutic, for after waking from their dreams, the characters find their troubles vanquished and their desires realized. This parallels the audience's experience of the play, which, like a confusing dream, still conveys a kind of truth.*

Throughout the middle scenes of the play we are repeatedly shown characters falling asleep and waking up. While they sleep on the stage, things happen around them, to them, in spite of them or oblivious to them. In most plays by Shakespeare—and indeed by most playwrights—characters not directly involved in the action are usually left off-stage; in *A Midsummer Night's Dream* they are just as likely to lie down on stage in full view of the audience and fall asleep. This has the double effect of removing characters from the action while keeping them in the eye of the audience: they are both there and not there. . . .

People sleep, people dream, and at the end of the night, magically, everything is sorted out. The descent into the wood, the place of the unconscious, the place of dreams, is itself a therapeutic process. Even without the benefit of psychoanalysis [for 'Man is but an ass if he go about t'expound this dream' (IV, i, l.

dreams at all, thanks to Oberon's kindness in turning all 'this night's accidents' into 'the fierce vexation of a dream' (4.1.67–8). All the lovers will have, apart from finding each other, will be their curiously coinciding dreams, 'all their minds transfigured so together', as Hippolyta puts it (5.1.24). She perceives it as 'something of great constancy' (l. 26), as Bottom will find his dream something he cannot begin to explain but whose awesome scale he is only too well aware of.

Throughout this introduction one of my major concerns has been the metamorphic processes of the play. *A Midsummer Night's Dream* is endlessly fascinated by the possibilities of transformation and translation within its action and by its metamorphoses of its materials. The richness of its fascination has been finely explored by [Leonard] Barkan and others. But where in Ovid metamorphosis is the final consequence of the narrative, in *A Midsummer Night's Dream* it initiates action. Barkan's emphasis that 'Shakespeare is more interested in transformation as a cause than transformation as an effect'

204)] characters find that their desires can be accommodated to social reality. Hermia and Lysander find that the obstacle to their love has been removed; Demetrius, much to his surprise, finds that he loves Helena better than Hermia after all. . . .

In Puck's final Epilogue the audience's experience of the play they have just seen as a whole is explicitly likened to that of a dream:

> If we shadows have offended,
> Think but this, and all is mended:
> That you have but slumbered here,
> While these visions did appear;
> And this weak and idle theme,
> No more yielding but a dream . . .

Epilogue, ll. 1–6

Puck's apparent dismissal of dreams as 'weak and idle', and yielding nothing, is ironic; throughout the play the audience has been shown repeatedly the 'truth' which resides in dreams. Now, by extension, the same truth-value is attributed to the stage. 'Bottom's Dream' is also ours, and it has been made not into a ballad by Peter Quince but into a play by William Shakespeare. The play which continually argues for the truth of dreams argues also for the truth of the stage.

Michael Mangan, *A Preface to Shakespeare's Comedies: 1594–1603*. London and New York: Longman, 1996, 159–61.

is reflected in the significance of sleep as the greatest, the most profound and unknowable of all transformative states. [William C.] Carroll's recognition that 'the metamorphs in the play notice nothing' is epitomized by this state of sleep. We cannot consciously know that we are asleep, though we can be strangely aware that we are dreaming. Sleep in *A Midsummer Night's Dream* is the embodiment for unknowing metamorphosis, dream the most complete state of transformed existence that we ever, let alone nightly, undergo.

It is in the process of recall of metamorphosis that *A Midsummer Night's Dream* distinguishes between the mortals. As Carroll observes, 'Only Bottom experiences metamorphosis, finally, by *remembering* it, though he was unaware of it at the time; the four lovers shrug it off like a hangover.' Yet even the hangover involves transfiguration, as Hippolyta recognizes. Living with one's dreams is never an easy process.

A Reflective Plot Structure

David P. Young

The pairing of many characters in *A Midsummer Night's Dream* lends unity and symmetry to the plot, while it also underscores thematic issues, in the view of scholar David P. Young. The confusing experiences of the four young lovers as they attempt to "pair off" serves to emphasize the impersonality of irrational love. The two royal pairs of characters also reflect versions of mature love. The mechanicals may be the most reflective characters in the play by virtue of the play they perform, a play that forces the audience into a broader awareness than that demonstrated by the courtly audience of Theseus.

There are two worlds in *A Midsummer Night's Dream*—the kingdom of Theseus and the kingdom of Oberon, the one an orderly society, the other a confusing wilderness. The action of the play moves between the two, as two groups of characters from the real and reasonable world find themselves temporarily lost in the imaginary and irrational world. This pattern of action corresponds closely both to the religious morality and the romance, where the respective heroes often move on a narrative line that can be schematized as follows:

Morality:

fall from grace / temporary prosperity of evil / divine reconciliation

Romance:

separation / wandering / reunion

As the secular drama came to supersede the religious, it branched out, and one of the variations, based on the pastoral ideal, presented the movement through bad fortune to good fortune in spheres of action already familiar from the romance:

Excerpted from David P. Young, *Something of Great Constancy: The Art of* A Midsummer Night's Dream. Copyright © 1966 by Yale University. Reprinted with permission from Yale University Press.

Pastoral Romance:
   society   /   wilderness   /   an improved society

The purest examples of this pattern in Shakespeare are *As You Like It* and the late romances, *Cymbeline, The Winter's Tale,* and *The Tempest,* but it may be found at work in plays as diverse as *Two Gentlemen* and *King Lear.* In *A Midsummer Night's Dream* it is present at its most comic pitch: the danger which initially sends the central characters into the wilderness is less severe than in, say, *As You Like It,* and the corresponding need for some sort of social reform is slight. The wilderness, as a result, comes to play a more dominant role. In the pastoral romances, it is usually a pseudo-ideal and a temporary haven. In *A Midsummer Night's Dream,* as personified in the fairies, it governs most of the action and controls most of the characters, recalling the more powerful forces of disruption at work in the midsection of both morality and romance.

CONCENTRIC CIRCLES

It will be noted that the spheres of action in these traditional narrative patterns do nor alter significantly. It is the characters and, by imaginative extension, ourselves who alter as we move through the worlds in question, discovering their interaction. In *A Midsummer Night's Dream,* this process of discovery reveals that the opposing worlds seem to form concentric circles. At first, following the characters from Athens to the woods, we may feel that the two areas are simply adjacent, but as Theseus and daylight reenter the play, we realize that it is possible to enter the woods and reemerge on the other side into human society. Thus, Theseus and his world seem to envelop the world of the woods. But Oberon and Titania, as we learn early in the play and are reminded directly at the end, are not the subjects of Theseus. Their awareness exceeds his, and their world is larger, enveloping his; he is their unconscious subject. Thus we discover another and larger circle, enclosing the first two. Then comes Puck's epilogue, which reminds us that everything we have been watching is a play, an event in a theater with ourselves as audience. Here is a still larger circle, enveloping all the others. The process stops there, but the discovery of ever more comprehensive circles inevitably suggests that there is another one still to be discovered. This is not merely a trick or a display of artistic ingenuity; treating us as it does

to an expansion of consciousness and a series of epistemo-
logical discoveries, it suggests that our knowledge of the
world is less reliable than it seems.

Thus it is that the concentric circles described above can
also be used to depict the spectrum of awareness formed by
the characters in the play. These are more usually depicted
as levels on a kind of rising ladder of intelligence and consciousness, but the very action by which we learn of the differences, that of one character standing aside to watch characters who are less aware of a given situation, suggests the
enclosing image of a circle or sphere. In the inmost circle
are the mechanicals, and at their center stands Bottom,
supremely ignorant of all that is happening. All of the humor
derived from Bottom depends on his absolute lack of awareness joined to the absolute confidence with which he moves
through the play. If this makes him amusing, it also makes
him sympathetic, as if we unconsciously recognized his kinship not only with the other characters but with ourselves.
The difference, after all, is one of degree.

In the next circle belong the lovers; they are not much better off than the clowns, but the fact that they are largely victims of enchantment rather than native stupidity gives them
claim to a fuller awareness, since Bottom's enchantment
never alters his behavior or his nature. The circle beyond
belongs to Theseus and Hippolyta, who oversee the action
from a distance and are not victimized by the fairies. Hippolyta deserves the further station, on the basis of her conversation with Theseus at the beginning of the fifth act. The
fairies occupy the next circle, Titania first, because she is
tricked by her husband, then Oberon and Puck. Even these
two, however, are not at all times fully aware of the course
of events, and we, the audience, watch them as they watch
the others. The furthest circle, then, belongs to us. Or is it the
furthest? Does not the playwright belong still further out,
overseeing not only the events of the play but our reaction to
them, enchanting us as Puck enchants the lovers?

SPATIAL CONSCIOUSNESS

The four groups into which the characters of *A Midsummer
Night's Dream* fall present us with another spatial aspect of
construction. The effect is like that of a fugue, in which we
are simultaneously aware of several lines of movement and
thus of position and interaction. Each of the four groups in

the play has its own set of experiences. Since we know that these are occurring simultaneously, we are conscious of the location of each group and the ways in which the various actions impinge upon one another. This consciousness is essentially spatial; it requires harmonious resolution just as does the temporal action. If for no other reason, the fairies' entrance in the fifth act would be necessary as the final step in the series of group positionings. The other three groups have gathered there; the arrival of the fairies completes the choreography. . . .

Our sense of the lovers' permutations, for example, is distinctly spatial; almost any discussion of them is apt to resort to diagrammatic figures. We begin the play with a triangle, Lysander-Hermia-Demetrius, but we soon realize, as Helena's presence and importance is established, that it is in fact a quadrangle, with Helena the neglected corner. In the second act, Lysander's allegiance is suddenly switched, so that we have "cross-wooing," each man pursuing the wrong woman. We also have, as Baldwin points out, a circle, since each of the four parties is pursuing another: Hermia is looking for Lysander; he is wooing Helena; she continues to love Demetrius; and he is still enamored of Hermia. This is the quadrangle at its most disrupted state, and two steps are necessary to repair it. The first of these comes in the third act, when Demetrius is restored to Helena. This reverses the original triangle, and Hermia becomes the neglected party. The fourth act finds the quadrangle in its proper state, each man attached to the right woman, restoring a situation which predates the beginning of the play.

These permutations are further complicated by the question of friendship. Each member of the quadrangle has, potentially, one love and two friends therein, but the shifting of love relationships disrupts the friendships as well. Lysander and Hermia are at the outset alienated from Demetrius but friends of Helena, so much so that they tell her their secret. When Lysander falls in love with Helena, their friendship is of course destroyed; she thinks he is making fun of her. The next alteration, Demetrius' restoration to Helena, destroys the Hermia-Helena friendship: Hermia thinks Helena is somehow responsible; Helena thinks everyone is mocking her. Thus, the restoration of the proper love relationships also restores the friendships of all four; even Lysander and Demetrius, who were ready to fight to the death, are friends again at the end of the play.

The lovers' quadrangle is set within another calmer quadrangle involving the royal couples. We learn of its existence when Oberon and Titania meet. She immediately charges him with love of Hippolyta, "Your buskin'd mistress and your warrior love," and he counters:

> How canst thou thus, for shame, Titania,
> Glance at my credit with Hippolyta,
> Knowing I know thy love to Theseus?

$$(\text{II}.1.74\text{--}76)$$

There are cross-purposes, it appears, within this group as well. They do not, however, lead to the complications that beset the lovers. Theseus and Hippolyta are unaware of the fairies' marital difficulties. Moreover, the true occasion of the quarrel is the changeling boy, so that Oberon's practicing on Titania is all that is needed to restore the quadrangle to harmony and enable the fairies to join forces for the ritual blessing at the end. . . .

REFLECTIONS AND SYMMETRY

We have already noticed the paired characters in *A Midsummer Night's Dream* and noted how they lend symmetry to the plot. Shakespeare also takes advantage of them to set up reflections which underline key dramatic ideas. Thus, the near-identity of the lovers is used to stress the inadequacy of that kind of love which yields itself to irrationality and the consequent heavy demands upon both personality and intelligence. Demetrius and Lysander address the women they woo in the same conventional vocabulary of exaggerated praise, each mirroring the other's inadequacy. The women expose one another in similar fashion. Hermia has no sooner sworn her love by Cupid's bow and arrow and by "all the vows that ever men have broke" than Helena is on stage for her soliloquy, talking of winged Cupid and Demetrius' broken oaths in the same way. Thus, the two women who think themselves so different—one lucky in love, the other rejected—are shown to have an identity which, incidentally, foreshadows the events to come. Later on, in the woods, Helena herself employs the image of a mirror. Speaking of her earlier desire to be like Hermia, she accounts herself a failure:

> What wicked and dissembling glass of mine,
> Made me compare with Hermia's sphery eyne?

$$(\text{II}.2.98\text{--}99)$$

It is at precisely this moment that Lysander wakes up and falls in love with her. "Transparent Helena," he shouts, not seeing in her the image of his folly. He too goes on to insist that she and Hermia are completely different. Throughout the night, the four lovers will peer at each other and always fail to see what the playwright makes so clear to us, their likenesses.

Much the same thing can be said about the royal pairs. It is appropriate that Theseus, as representative of daylight and right reason, should have subdued his bride-to-be to the rule of his masculine will. That is the natural order of things. It is equally appropriate that Oberon, as king of darkness and fantasy, should have lost control of his wife, and that the corresponding natural disorder described by Titania should ensue. All the details in these dual situations have the same function. Both royal pairs love panoramas, but the landscapes they see are appropriately different. The means that each king employs to establish rule in his kingdom are significantly opposed. Even the Masters of the Revels of each monarchy, Philostrate and Puck, serve to strengthen the sense of contrast within likeness. . . .

If any group of characters in the play may be said to exist primarily for purposes of reflection, it is the mechanicals. This does not subordinate them in importance; they could easily claim supreme position as the busiest glasses in this comedy of reflection. What is more, they bring to the climax of the play its biggest and funniest mirror. Their reflective function is worth examining in some detail.

THE MECHANICALS' REFLECTIVE FUNCTION

The mechanicals' first scene gives us hints of the echo and parody we are to have from them through the rest of the play. Their concern for an orderly handling of their task catches the theme Theseus has just sounded and will continue to sound throughout the play. Their respect for hierarchy recalls the issue raised by the entrance of Egeus and the lovers, and their plans for rehearsal echo the plans of Demetrius and Hermia. Their confused use of language (e.g. "I will aggravate my voice") presents an aspect of the confusion that will later reign in the woods, and the paradoxes they blunder into, "lamentable comedy," "monstrous little voice," hint at the doubts about familiar categories—dreaming and waking, reason and imagination—with which the play will eventually leave us. The interlude about true love they plan to perform promises to mock the lovers we have just seen. . . .

"Pyramus and Thisby" is the climax of the mechanicals' reflective career. If it does not succeed in holding the mirror up to nature, it holds it up to almost everything else. "The best in this kind are but shadows," says Theseus. Shadows of what? Of the events and characters of *A Midsummer Night's Dream*, but the audience of "Pyramus and Thisby" may be partially pardoned for not recognizing their own images. The lovers, back from the woods and safely married, need not compare their experiences with those of Pyramus and Thisby in a less accommodating wood. Nor can they be expected so soon to recognize in the poetry of the play the inadequate language of their own vocabulary of love. Theseus and Hippolyta, too, have put their pasts behind them; nothing about this play is able to provoke their memories. The mechanicals, as with the other effects of the drama, fail in this function too; "speculation turns not to itself."

Not, that is, among the characters of the play. But we are also the audience of "Pyramus and Thisby" and have many comparisons to make. The resemblance between the "fond pageant" in the woods and the "tragical mirth" in the palace does not escape us, nor do the references to at least some of the other plays and the various dramatic and poetic conventions which the playwright finds hard to admire. Beyond these reflections we begin to discern an even larger one. Perhaps it is begun by Theseus' remarks about the poet, but it is the kind of insight that ought to be provoked by any play within a play, a mirror for the audience—drama relationship if ever there was one. Shakespeare exploits it thoroughly. Within a play about love written for a wedding, he puts a play about love written for a wedding. . . .

The discerning audience will finally find in the mirror of the mechanicals' performance one more image—its own. They are bound to notice that "Pyramus and Thisby" does not have a very perceptive audience. Not that it deserves one, but as *A Midsummer Night's Dream* is superior to "Pyramus and Thisby," so, the playwright seems to hope, will its audience be superior. Elizabethan audiences, we know, were not always as attentive or polite as the actors and playwrights might wish. Perhaps they were being asked in this comedy, as well as in *Love's Labour's Lost*, to recognize their image and reform it altogether. Certainly they are given a chance to behave more astutely than the audience of "Pyramus and Thisby," to see to it that they are not quite as condescending as Theseus, as inconsistent as Hippolyta, as oblivious, when faced with their own images, as the lovers. The playwright, by placing them higher than any of the characters in the play, gives them every opportunity. If they should fail, they have only themselves to blame. There is just a hint of mockery in Puck's epilogue:

> If we shadows have offended,
> Thinke but this, and all is mended—
> That you have but slumb'red here
> While these visions did appear.
> And this weak and idle theme,
> No more yielding but a dream.

>   (V.1.430–35)

Anyone who is willing to admit that he has slept through this performance cannot claim to be very alert. In fact, he must inevitably be compared to those characters in the play who are willing to think that they have "dreamed" it, dismissing events which exposed them significantly. Shakespeare gives us our choice. We may remain within the outer circles of consciousness with Oberon, Puck, and himself, or we may doze off and fall inward toward the condition of Bottom and the lovers. In the mirror of *A Midsummer Night's Dream*, the spectator may find, even if he does not recognize, his very form and pressure.

Intellectual Polarities

Peter Hollindale

There is a pervasive symmetry in the pairing of characters and in the overall structure of *A Midsummer Night's Dream*. This organizational scheme can also be discerned in a set of intellectual symmetries around the play's main ideas, according to Peter Hollindale, senior lecturer in English at York University. Sleep and waking, reason and imagination, reason and love are important intellectual polarities unifying the structure of the play. Hollindale argues that the play celebrates a kind of creative antagonism between different yet complementary ways of knowing our world and ourselves.

The symmetry of composition which is so conspicuous a feature of *A Midsummer Night's Dream* extends beyond language, character and dramatic structure to the systematic ordering of ideas. The play is built around a set of opposites, dualities or polarities which play against each other. Pairs are important throughout. There are two pairs of lovers and two pairs of royal personages, with oppositional relationships at different stages of resolution in each pair. There are two locales, Athens and the wood, the first representing an enclosed, confined and courtly space, the second an open, frontierless and rural one. There are the paired opposites of day and night, light and darkness, sun and moon. The natural inhabitants of the contrasted worlds are opposite in bodily form, the Athenian being solidly physical and, in the persons of Bottom and the mechanicals, gross and heavy, and the woodland figures being light and graceful and, in the persons of the smallest fairies, delicate and airy. The Athenians are mortal, the fairies are immortal. Opposed and contrasted pairings are thus as clear as may be, in the setting and the atmosphere of the play, in character-groups and character-relationships. A similar patterning of opposites can be found in the play's more abstract conditions and ideas.

This systematic binary organization can seem too regular, too contrived and over-cerebral, if we look at it purely as a static phenomenon imprinted on the play, and there is certainly no reason to suppose that the young Shakespeare did not get pleasure from his neatness of design. Static, however, is the least appropriate word for *A Midsummer Night's Dream*. . . . The play is continually in motion, and all the pairings are continually changing their relationship or dominance. At some of the most powerful moments in the drama, two worlds briefly meet, or overlap, or just avoid each other. A summer's dawn is common ground between day and night, light and dark, Theseus and Oberon, waking and sleeping, and in the transitory half-light there are glimpses of a twofold truth; so Hermia can say

> Methinks I see these things with parted eye,
> When everything seems double.
>
> (IV.i.188–9)

A more extraordinary and grotesque encounter between two opposed realities is the relationship of Titania and Bottom, a relationship between immortal and mortal, high and low, ethereal and animal, delicate and gross. Within the relationships there is similar mobility and flux, barely traceable in the state of affairs between Theseus and Hippolyta, but not completely non-existent, and very obvious indeed in the quarrel and reconciliation of Oberon and Titania, and the fluctuating passions of the lovers. As their emotions and fidelities are in processes of change, so are their bodies in movement. So omnipresent is the paired activity that the play's few single figures—Egeus, Philostrate, Puck—stand out as oddities, and only Puck takes on the extra transcendental quality of wholly self-contained, autonomous life. Even he takes evident delight in the comic pattern of doubleness. As he collects the lovers for their final dispositions, the arithmetic neatness is a joke to him:

> Yet but three? Come one more,
> Two of both kinds makes up four.
>
> (III.ii.437–8)

Matrimony—the association of man and woman as two who become one, and yet remain two—is the principal subject of the play. It is also, however, the paradigm of the relationship of pairs, the symbolic condition to which other dualities or polarities aspire. In marriage, opposites combine; they merge to become one thing, one flesh, but they also complement each other in two separate bodies, their creative and joyous antagonism leading to procreation and new life. In addition to all its other felicities, the place of marriage in *A Midsummer Night's Dream* can only be fully understood if it is seen as intellectually pleasing, the most comprehensive mathematical harmonization of two and one.

SLEEPING AND WAKING

Nothing else in the play's arrangement of duets can measure up to that, but the play consistently 'marries' opposites and abstractions in comparable ways. Most important of these, perhaps, is the marriage of sleeping and waking. At the end of the play all the mortals go off to lovemaking and sleep, guarded by the wakeful fairies. Before this night of ordered harmony, the previous night of trials in the wood has been marked by a great deal of sleeping. Titania sleeps, Bottom sleeps, all the lovers sleep—Lysander and Hermia sleep twice. Their emergence from these sleeps is usually a switch to instantaneous, charged, traumatic wakefulness, a sudden stroke of passion or bewilderment. The two conditions are diametrically opposed, but somewhere between them is the enigma of the dream. Dream is the child of sleep, but in fact the play has only one sleeping dream, Hermia's at the end of Act II scene ii, and even her dream is symbolic of the state to which she wakes. Everything else that the characters subsequently call a dream is what we, the audience, know to have been a wide-awake experience.

The best extensive discussion of the nature of dream in this play and in Elizabethan thought is David P. Young's. He demonstrates the low regard in which dreams were held in the period, and their association with insubstantiality and illusion elsewhere in Shakespeare. Dreams in popular belief were shadowy, misleading and undependable, and to awake from dreaming was to awake from illusion into truth. This is certainly what Theseus thinks when he hears the story of the lovers' recollections, though Hippolyta is much less sure. But the nature of dream in this play is much less simple. Young observes, 'Shakespeare's characteristic practice with something like the dreaming-waking polarity is to question both concepts, turning them against each other until they acquire a paradoxical relationship,' and he notes that it is the stupid Bottom who responds most accurately to his supposed dream experience on waking.

In *A Midsummer Night's Dream*, the characters' dreams are only illusions in the contextual sense that the play which frames them is illusion. In so far as the play is a fiction, and the audience is conscious of theatrical illusion, then the dreams are illusion within an illusion, and the play's title describes the audience's experience; in so far as we provisionally acquiesce through our imagination to the play as 'true', then the dreams of the characters are waking dreams, living experiences, and 'true'. In the end, the truth of dream is inseparable from imagination, art and theatrical 'truth'. The night-time experiences cannot be dismissed *within* the play, as Theseus tries to do, because he is mistaken. They can only be dismissed by references external to the play, and if we do that we risk 'doing a Theseus'. At one level we are ourselves experiencing dramatic illusion, or a waking dream.

THE IMAGERY OF MOON AND WATER

As scholars have noted over the years, A Midsummer Night's Dream *is a powerfully unified play, though its unity is not due to traditional notions of plot structure. Rather, its unity is achieved through parallel characters, parallel situations, recurring themes, and pairs of ideas. Further, as Mark Van Doren notes, a subtle but powerful kind of unity is also achieved through the poetry of the play, especially in the recurrent imagery of the moon and water.*

The poetry of the play is dominated by the words moon and water. Theseus and Hippolyta carve the moon in our memory with the strong, fresh strokes of their opening dialogue:

THESEUS.   Now, fair Hippolyta, our nuptial hour
            Draws on apace. Four happy days bring in
            Another moon; but, O, methinks, how slow
            This old moon wanes! She lingers my desires,
            Like to a step-dame or a dowager
            Long withering out a young man's revenue.
HIPPOLYTA. Four days will quickly steep themselves in night;
            Four nights will quickly dream away the time;
            And then the moon, like to a silver bow
            New-bent in heaven, shall behold the night
            Of our solemnities.

This is not the sensuous, softer orb of "Antony and Cleopatra," nor is it the sweet sleeping friend of Lorenzo and Jessica. It is

Like Theseus, the audience can choose between consenting imaginatively to the improbable story we are told or dismissing it as illusion and dream. But the difference between waking and sleeping is a crucial one. Its sharply articulated opposition within the play is therefore a means to open up more searching questions about the nature of dream and 'truth'. In answering questions his play poses, it is arguable that even Shakespeare was not fully in possession of the terms he needed. . . . This discussion may illustrate the truth of Young's point, that the polarity (which in my view lies between sleeping and waking rather than between dreaming and waking) is the means to open up paradox and intellectual challenge. It creates the space for a different idea of dream—the waking dream, or the dream which embodies a coexistent truth. This idea, situated between the polarities of sleep and waking, questions the established categories and judgements, and denies the limits set by Theseus.

---

brilliant and brisk, silver-distant, and an occasion for comedy in Theseus's worldy thought. Later on in the same scene he will call it cold and fruitless (73), and Lysander will look forward to

> Tomorrow night, when Phoebe doth behold
> Her silver visage in the watery glass,
> Decking with liquid pearl the bladed grass.   (I, i, 209–11)

Lysander has connected the image of the moon with the image of cool water on which it shines, and hereafter they will be inseparable. "A Midsummer Night's Dream" is drenched with dew when it is not saturated with rain. A film of water spreads over it, enhances and enlarges it miraculously. The fairy whom Robin hails as the second act opens wanders swifter than the moon's sphere through fire and flood. The moon, says Titania, is governess of floods, and in anger at Oberon's brawls has sucked up from the sea contagious fogs, made every river overflow, drowned the fields and rotted the green corn:

> The nine men's morris is fill'd up with mud,
> And the quaint mazes in the wanton green
> For lack of tread are undistinguishable.   (II, i, 98–100)

Here in the west there has been a deluge, and every object still drips moisture.

Mark Van Doren, *Shakespeare.* Garden City, NY: Doubleday, 1953.

REASON AND IMAGINATION

The second of the play's great intellectual polarities is that between reason and imagination. Theseus' famous speech at the beginning of Act V scene i is again the conceptual centrepiece of the play, but in giving it that status it is important not to treat it as an authoritative statement which enjoys some kind of choric dependability external to the play. It is a speech within the play, made by a thoughtful, intelligent and rational character who is nevertheless fallible. Just as his scepticism about the believability of reported 'dreams' is seen to be fallible, because he is under-informed and has not seen what we have, so his more inclusive statement about the respective status of reason and imagination may prove to be both partial and inadequate.

Shakespeare's exploration of the polarities in this play often works from a starting-point where there is some ambivalence in the more contentious of the two opposites. Wakefulness is presumed to be trustworthy and dream illusory, but sleep, the normal habitation of dream, is in itself necessary and good. Likewise reason is presumed to be dependable and estimable. The high eminence of reason in Elizabethan hierarchic thinking is beyond dispute. We have already seen that the lovers try to justify their irrational behaviour by constructing plausible frameworks of reason to support themselves, and even the thick-skin Bottom, when he observes that love and reason keep little company nowadays, is in no doubt that they ought to. There is no question of demoting reason from its earned and justified high status in this contest of polarities, or that Theseus is a commendable figure who defends it. Rather the question which is raised is whether reason is sufficient in itself to account for all experience, or whether there are parts of life which need other terms of understanding.

Here imagination is in a similar position to that of sleep and dream. In contemporary Elizabethan thinking the status of imagination was lower than that of reason, and its proper place lay within a system of relativities. Imagination is not wrong or undesirable in itself, but undesirable if it displaces reason from its position of primary authority, becoming out of hand, excessive and ungovernable. Pejorative references to imagination (in Shakespeare as elsewhere) are customarily to *uncontrolled* imagination. Allowed unlicensed range beyond the constraints of reason, imagination could liberate interior conditions of disorder, which may then take external forms such as passion, anarchy or madness. Imagination's true place lay in ordered hierarchical subjection to the higher faculty of reason, acting as an intermediary agent between the rational powers and the senses. When Theseus in his great speech sets reason and imagination in opposition to each other, he is not considering them as equals. The unfortunate position of imagination was that it was almost bound to lose in one or other of two ways: either it was too closely tied to the senses, and therefore too prone to sensory distraction from the authority of reason, or it was too free of affiliations either to reason or the senses, and therefore liable to generate illusions by its unconfined activity.

Against this suspect and subordinate placement, however, must be set the powers and qualities that imagination could be allowed. Imagination was not only a receptive agency for the impressions which the senses supplied, but the faculty by which they were stored, arranged and valued. It therefore has several potential roles which endow it with respectability and importance, to set against its junior and potentially disordering relationship with reason. It provides the rational powers with a source of knowledge derived from sensory experience; it has a 'shaping' or 'making' quality which is itself a creative action exerted upon sensory data, and it has autonomous generative capabilities which could be viewed with something less than complete scepticism and distrust. What matters in relation to the thought-patterns of *A Midsummer Night's Dream* is above all the fact that imagination was a concept surrounded by contentious uncertainty and possible contradictions, rather than fixed evaluative judgement.

In Theseus's speech, imagination is set in paired and oppositional relationship to reason, but is also subdivided into subsidiary and constituent relationships. In these the uncertainties described above are clearly detectable. Theseus finds imagination at large in three groups:

> The lunatic, the lover and the poet
> Are of imagination all compact.
> (V.i.7–8)

Reason, that is to say, is set in several oppositional pairings under the umbrella of imagination. The pairings are reason and madness, reason and love, reason and poetry. Little analysis is needed to see that these subordinate antitheses make it impossible to give to imagination a single function or meaning or value. Madness is diametrically opposed to reason and true judgement: it is irrational, illusory and false, especially in relation to excess. The madman not only sees devils, but unrealistic numbers of them. The lover ('all as frantic' according to Theseus, but not according to his better-informed audience) sees 'Helen's beauty in a brow of Egypt', and in so doing asserts an alternative perception, a different process of knowing and judging, from the customary one. Love has its own mode of judgement, not easily brought into consonance with the accepted public one and (as we have seen in the case of the lovers) deeply unconvincing when it tries to be so. Down-to-earth Bottom sees at once the absurdity of Titania's passion for him, and tells her so:

> ... Reason and love keep little company together nowadays—
> the more the pity that some honest neighbours will not make
> them friends.
>
> (III.i.136–8)

This is not to say that love is inherently and irredeemably irrational, however. Love is capable of a madness of unreason and incongruity *at times*; Titania's contrived adoration of Bottom is a visible and hilarious example of love as a madness, and Lysander's Act I duet with Hermia laments other forms. But love is not incompatible with reason, provided it observes its own internal rationales, and provided that external forces are amenable to the outcome of love's reason.

It is precisely such an achieved compatibility that *A Midsummer Night's Dream* celebrates. Its outcome is marriage, ... an integration of emotive and social, internal and external, measures. The fact of the play's love plot is that love and reason keep little company together in the antics of the love quartet, while they are left to their own devices. For a time, imagination in its form as love seems irretrievably at odds with reason, its madness expressed in volatile, impulsive, irrational behaviour and also in failed efforts to use reason as an aid to self-excuse. This love quartet are in luck, however (in contrast, for example, to Romeo and Juliet): they have honest neighbours to make love and reason friends. One honest neighbour is Oberon, who uses magical powers to correct the subjective irrationalities of passion and restore the symmetrical harmony which existed before Demetrius' madness. The other honest neighbour is Theseus, who intervenes to correct the social irrationality represented by Egeus. With the aid of these two honest neighbours, two and two can make up four.

Theseus knows nothing of Oberon, though, and his analysis is incomplete. It reaches only as far as his own fiefdom of benevolence. Because of our own superior knowledge, we in the audience know that Oberon's role is equal to that of Theseus in achieving the lovers' happiness. Imagination-as-love is therefore vindicated beyond Theseus' power to know it. Imagination and Reason, in the persons of the complementary potentates, are given dramatic equity of status in the achievement of socially acceptable and successful marriages.

REASON AND POETRY

The third subordinate pairing is that of reason and poetry. The quality which Theseus perceives in the poet's imagination is different again. It is neither the anarchic destruction of external order which afflicts the madman, nor the operation of a different judgemental function, unstable if devoid of complementary reason, as with the lover, but the autonomous generative faculty which, as set out above, was one of imagination's possible roles. The poet gives shapes to transparencies of air, as indeed the play itself does in its movement from the creative mind to the complex duality of illusion and reality which is stage performance. In speaking of 'airy nothing', Theseus is inadequate. Shakespeare is notable for his ironic preoccupation with the word 'nothing' (above all in *King Lear*) and his cautious refusal to concede the absolute nothingness of 'nothing'. In this speech 'nothing' is Theseus' concept, not Shakespeare's. The process of shaping and naming which Theseus airily dismisses is precisely the creative energy of theatre and of art. Theseus' dismissal of the poet is undercut by his position as an airy nothing given place and name in the play we are watching.

The speech, therefore, contrary to what Theseus 'intends' by it, is a conditional but powerful vindication of imagination's complementary and equal role with reason in the dialectic of understanding. In order to understand it we have to make our own adjustments, prompted by the text, to the way we think about the meaning of 'imagination', just as we did with the meaning of 'dream'. Within the speech we have a further conceptual prompting contained in the words 'apprehend' and 'comprehend'. Designedly, the two words are repeated in conceptual proximity. Apprehension is the province of imagination, comprehension the province of reason. The irrational ones have

> . . . shaping fantasies, that apprehend
> More than cool reason ever comprehends
> (V.i.5–6)

and the imagination of these characters plays tricks:

> That if it would but apprehend some joy,
> It comprehends some bringer of that joy. . . .
> (V.i.19–20)

'Comprehension' in this context is most precisely defined not as 'complete understanding' but as 'rational inference'; while 'apprehension' is more accurately defined as 'intuitive perception'. Theseus is not mixing up the meaning of his terms but misapplying their relative values. His seeming confusion about imagination's response to joy consists in supposing that only by rational inference can it be understood. When the imagination is moved by joy, its understanding of a 'bringer' is a function of intelligent perception *in itself,* not of some illusory rational continuum. The effect (contrary to what Theseus is arguing) is to assert the intelligence of imagination in its own right, as a way of knowing which complements reason but does not require to be ratified by it.

Thus Theseus' brilliantly argued error affirms by its confident inadequacies the intellectual structure of the play, which is a celebration of doubleness, of complementary ways of knowing. Their value may lie in mutual necessity and the creative antagonism which exists between them, or in their mergence and fusion. The central event and central image of marriage is both these things. It is surrounded by a set of others, some of which are discussed above: sleep and waking, imagination and reason, art and nature, illusion and truth, licence and order, shadow and substance, the theatre and the world. The clarity of these oppositions allows the play to explore the space between them, to examine the terms themselves and also the intermediate terms which are used, or missing, or needed, or suspectly defined. Between the stasis of the opposites there is ceaseless intellectual mobility. If this sounds cerebral and abstract for a play, we only need to remind ourselves of the dance—the restless mobility of bodies, the vivid physicality of the play; its intellectual design is expressed through means which are wholly theatrical.

The Ending of the Play

Anne Barton

The final act of *A Midsummer Night's Dream* is
highly unusual, according to scholar Anne Barton,
professor of English at Cambridge University, for all
the tensions and entanglements of the lovers' es-
capades are resolved by the end of the fourth act.
The only unresolved plot strand is the performance
of the play by Bottom and his mechanicals. Act Five,
then, becomes both an extended commentary on the
action that has preceded it and a relaxed interroga-
tion of the relationship between art and life. According to Barton, Shakespeare enables us to understand
more of this relationship than the play's courtly audience, for we see the parallels between Pyramus
and Thisbe and the young lovers. We also see the
play's tragedy transformed into farce in the hands of
Bottom and his men, echoing the transformation of
the lovers' situation from potential tragedy to joy.

The last act of *A Midsummer Night's Dream* is concerned
principally, and even somewhat self-consciously, with the
relationship between art and life, dreams and the waking
world. In terms of plot, this fifth act is superfluous. Almost
all the business of the comedy has been concluded at the
end of Act IV: the error of Titania's vision put right and she
herself reconciled with Oberon, Hermia paired off happily
with Lysander and Helena with Demetrius. Theseus has not
only overruled the objections of old Egeus, but insisted upon
associating these marriages with his own: "Away with us to
Athens. Three and three, / We'll hold a feast in great solemnity" (IV.i.184–85). This couplet has the authentic ring of a
comedy conclusion. Only one expectation generated by the
action remains unfulfilled: the presentation of the Pyramus
and Thisby play before the Duke and his bride. Out of this
single remaining bit of material, Shakespeare constructs a

fifth act which seems, in effect, to take place beyond the normal, plot-defined boundaries of comedy.

The new social order which has emerged from the ordeal of the wood makes its first public appearance at the performance of the mechanicals' play. It is sensitive and hopeful. Theseus, characteristically, is condescending about the actor's art: "The best in this kind are but shadows; and the worst are no worse, if imagination amend them" (V.i.211–12). Richard Burbage would scarcely have thanked him. Such a view of the theatre overstresses the audience's lordly willingness-to-be-fooled at the expense of the power of illusion. Certainly a quite extraordinary effort of imagination would be required to extract Aristotelian pity and fear from the tragedy of Pyramus and Thisby as enacted by Bottom and Flute. The courtly audience, like the theatre audience, laughs at the ineptitudes and absurdities of the play within the play. Unlike Berowne and his friends in the equivalent scene of *Love's Labor's Lost,* however, the on-stage spectators in *A Midsummer Night's Dream* remain courteous. Most of the remarks made by Theseus, Hippolyta, and the four lovers are not heard by the preoccupied actors. Those that do penetrate, suggestions as to the proper disposition of Moonshine's lantern, dog, and bush, cries of "Well roar'd, Lion" and "Well run, Thisby," are entirely in the spirit of the performance. It was Bottom, after all, back in the rehearsal stage, who fondly imagined a success for Lion so great that the audience would intervene to request an encore: "Let him roar again." Gratifyingly, this wish-dream just about comes true. As the play proceeds, tolerance ripens into geniality, into an unforced accord between actors and spectators based upon considerations far more complex than anything articulated by Theseus. Although the artistic merit of the Pyramus and Thisby play is virtually non-existent, the performance itself is a resounding success. No feelings have been hurt, and everyone has had a thoroughly good time. Even Theseus finds that "this palpable-gross play hath well beguil'd / The heavy gait of night" (V.i.367–68).

TRANSFORMING CALAMITY TO JOY

For the theatre audience, granted a perspective wider than the one enjoyed by Theseus and the members of his court, the Pyramus and Thisby story of love thwarted by parents and the enmity of the stars consolidates and in a sense defines the happy ending of *A Midsummer Night's Dream*. It reminds us of the initial dilemma of Hermia and Lysander, and also of how their story might well have ended: with blood and deprivation. The heavy rhetoric of the interlude fairly bristles with fate and disaster, introducing into Act V a massing of images of death. The entire action of the play within the play is tragic in intention, although not in execution. Without meaning to do so, Bottom and his associates transform tragedy into farce before our eyes, converting that litany of true love crossed which was rehearsed in the very first scene by Hermia and Lysander to laughter. In doing so, they recapitulate the development of *A Midsummer Night's Dream* as a whole, reenacting its movement from potential calamity to an ending in which quick bright things come not to confusion, as once seemed inevitable, but to joy. An intelligent director can and should ensure that the on-stage audience demonstrates some awareness of the ground-bass of mortality sounding underneath the hilarity generated by Bottom's performance, that a line like Lysander's "he is dead, he is nothing" (V.i.308–9) is not lost in the merriment. Only the theatre audience, however, can capture the full resonance of the Pyramus and Thisby play.

When Theseus dismisses the actors after the Bergomask, and the members of the stage audience depart to their chambers, *A Midsummer Night's Dream* seems once again to have arrived at its ending. For the second time Theseus is given a couplet which sounds like the last lines of a play (V.i.369–70). When something like this happened at the end of Act IV it was Bottom, starting up out of his sleep, who set the comedy going again. This time it is the entrance of the fairies, but again the prolongation has nothing to do with plot. The appearance of Puck, Oberon, Titania and their train in the heart of Athens lends a symmetry to the action which would otherwise have been lacking and also gives the lie to Theseus's scepticism. Most important of all, however, is the way Puck's speech picks up and transforms precisely those ideas of death and destruction distanced through laughter in the Pyramus and Thisby play.

> Now the hungry lion roars,
> And the wolf behowls the moon;
> Whilst the heavy ploughman snores,
> All with weary task foredone.
> Now the wasted brands do glow,

Whilst the screech-owl, screeching loud,
Puts the wretch that lies in woe
In remembrance of a shroud.
Now it is the time of night
That the graves, all gaping wide,
Every one lets forth his sprite,
In the church-way paths to glide.

All the images here are of sickness, toil, and death. Even the wasted brands, in context, suggest the inevitable running down of human life as it approaches the grave.

THE CHALLENGE TO THESEUS

Once again, Shakespeare has adjusted the balance between art and life, reality and illusion. Puck's hungry lion is something genuinely savage, not at all the "very gentle beast, and of a good conscience" (V.i.227–28) impersonated by Snug. Even so, his talk of graves and shrouds, drudgery and exhaustion, brings the sense of mortality kept at bay in the Pyramus and Thisby interlude closer, preparing us for the true end of the comedy after so many feints and false conclusions. Puck's speech begins a modulation which will terminate, some fifty lines later, in direct address to the audience and in a player's request for applause. Actors and spectators alike will be turned out of Athens to face the workaday world. Yet Shakespeare refuses to concede that Theseus was right. In the first place, Puck's account of the terrors of the night is not final. It serves to introduce Oberon and Titania, the most fantastic characters in the play, and in their hands Puck's night fears turn into benediction and blessing. About the facts of mortality themselves the fairy king and queen can do nothing, even as Titania could do nothing to prevent the death, years before, of the votaress of her order. All they can do is to strengthen the fidelity and trust of the three pairs of lovers, to bless these marriages, and to stress the positive side of the night as a time for love and procreation as well as for death and fear. Certainly the emphasis on the fair, unblemished children to be born is not accidental, something to be explained purely in terms of the possible occasion of the play's first performance. These children summoned up by Oberon extend the comedy into the future, counteracting the artificial finality which always threatens to diminish happy endings. A beginning is made implicit in the final moments of the play, a further and wider circle.

Unlike characters in fairy-tale, Theseus and Hippolyta, Demetrius and Helena, Lysander and Hermia cannot live happily ever after. Only the qualified immortality to be obtained through offspring is available to them. It was an idea of survival in time which the Shakespeare of the sonnets came to distrust. Nevertheless, in the general atmosphere of celebration and blessing at the end of *A Midsummer Night's Dream*, it seems for the moment enough. It is only after this final coming together in Theseus's palace of the two poles of the comedy, a world of fantasy and one of fact, of immortality and of death, that Puck turns to speak to the theatre audience. Like Theseus, he describes the actors as "shadows" and sums up the play now concluded as a "weak and idle theme, / No more yielding than a dream." When John Lyly ended his court comedies with superficially similar words of deprecation and apology, he seems to have meant them literally. Shakespeare is far more devious. Images of sleep and dreams, shadows and illusions, have been used so constantly in the course of the comedy, examined and invested with such body and significance that they cannot be regarded now as simple terms of denigration and dismissal. As with that mock-apology for the author's "rough and all-unable pen" which concludes *Henry V*, Shakespeare seems to have felt able to trust his audience to take the point: to recognize the simplification, and to understand that the play has created its own reality, a reality touching our own at every point which

> More witnesseth than fancy's images,
> And grows to something of great constancy;
> But howsoever, strange and admirable. (V.i.25–27)

CHAPTER 3

The Themes of *A Midsummer Night's Dream*

The Complexities
of Love

Catherine Belsey

A Midsummer Night's Dream is fundamentally a play
about love, according to scholar Catherine Belsey of the
University of Wales, Cardiff. But instead of trying to define love, the play seeks to dramatize the experience of
love through a variety of characters and voices. Idealis-
tic, romantic love, passionate, irrational love, urgent,
prosaic love, and jealous, controlling love—all are given
voice in the play. The play does enlist our sympathy for
the young lovers and their confused desires, but the play
ultimately portrays the nature of love as elusive and
mysterious. Through the reappearance of the fairies in
the court at play's end, the idea is refuted that some
kind of orderly, rational love can be distinctly maintained apart from the passionate, irrational side of love.

When Bottom wakes up, near the end of *A Midsummer Night's
Dream*, after spending a night of love with the queen of the
fairies, this formerly masterful and garrulous figure is suddenly very nearly inarticulate. What could he say that would do
justice to the experience? "I have had a most rare vision. I have
had a dream past the wit of man to say what dream it was. Man
is but an ass if he go about to expound this dream" (4.1.214–17).
Bottom's name, and his transformation—an event that clarifies
more than it changes his identity—invite the audience to asso-
ciate him with the least poetic aspects of life, and yet, even as an
ass, Bottom has been touched by something special but mysterious, a power that he finds unusually hard to define. In quest
of a way of talking about what has happened to him, Bottom
reaches for the language of the Bible, St. Paul's account of the
future glory that God has prepared for human beings (1
Corinthians 2.9), though of course, being Bottom, he gets it
wrong: "The eye of man hath not heard, the ear of man hath not

seen, man's hand is not able to taste, his tongue to conceive, nor his heart to report what my dream was" (4.1.220–24). In the end he concludes that the solution is for Peter Quince to write a ballad of his dream. Evidently only the lyricism of popular poetry seems to Bottom adequate to define the experience of love.

We do not have Peter Quince's ballad, but—if we assume that Quince wrote "Pyramus and Thisbe," in which Bottom plays the romantic hero—we do have his play, and we also have Shakespeare's play, which is its setting. *A Midsummer Night's Dream* is a play about love. It proposes that love is a dream, or perhaps a vision; that it is absurd, irrational, a delusion, or, perhaps, on the other hand, a transfiguration; that it is doomed to be momentary ("So quick bright things come to confusion" [1.1.151]), and that it constitutes at the same time the proper foundation for lifelong marriage. Possibly Bottom is right, the play suggests, not to pin down anything so multiple, not to encapsulate love in a neat definition that would encourage us to measure our own and other people's experience and find it normal or abnormal, mature or immature, wise or foolish. The play's device, on the contrary, is to dramatize the plurality of love by characterizing it differently in a range of distinct voices.

VARIATIONS OF LOVE

As soon as Hermia and Lysander are left alone together on the stage for the first time, they discuss their predicament in a series of elegant and elaborate exchanges:

LYSANDER
> How now, my love? Why is your cheek so pale?
> How chance the roses there do fade so fast?

HERMIA
> Belike for want of rain, which I could well
> Beteem them from the tempest of mine eyes.

(1.1.130–33)

Since the lovers and the audience have both heard Theseus tell Hermia that she must die or go into a convent if she refuses to marry another man, it is hardly necessary for Lysander to ask why she is pale, or for her to tell him that she thinks she might be going to cry. But the poetic image of the roses in her cheeks legitimates the conceit that follows: the roses are short of water, which Hermia is about to supply. The exchange has the effect of distancing the threat to Hermia, and putting before the audience instead what is delicate, lyrical, and witty in romance.

Lysander's next utterance explains the way all four lovers tend to talk to each other.

> Ay me! For aught that I could ever read,
> Could ever hear by tale or history . . .
>
> (1.1.134–35)

How else, after all, do people learn to talk about love in the first instance, except by reading love stories? No wonder the four lovers are virtually indistinguishable. Romantic love is in this sense oddly impersonal. Because of love's power to idealize, the object of desire seems unique, even though in the event it turns out that Hermia and Helena are interchangeable. But the ways of idealizing, of investing the other person with the special beauty or magnetism that justifies desire, are drawn in the first place from the culture in which people learn about love.

Meanwhile Theseus, we are to understand, in contrast to the young lovers, has been around. The stories of his many loves and betrayals would have been well known, at least to those members of the audience who had been to school, and Oberon alludes to them in the course of his quarrel with Titania (2.1.81–83). Theseus himself talks quite differently about love:

> Now, fair Hippolyta, our nuptial hour
> Draws on apace. Four happy days bring in
> Another moon. But, O, methinks how slow
> This old moon wanes! She lingers my desires
> Like to a stepdame or a dowager
> Long withering out a young man's revenue.
>
> (1.1.1–6)

Theseus acknowledges that he has desires, and they are urgent and imperative. He is impatient with the moon, that conventional poetic symbol of romance, and the comparison he invokes is anything but lyrical. The moon that is delaying his marriage is like an old woman who refuses to die and so prevents her young heir from getting his hands on his inheritance. Paradoxically, the love that is voiced by Theseus seems more insistent to the degree that it is more prosaic, literally more like prose, since the speech rhythms do not coincide with the line endings, but run directly across them. The Amazon Hippolyta, whose comments so often counterpoint those of Theseus, immediately supplies the missing romance by reinvesting with its customary lyricism "the moon, like to a silver bow / New-bent in heaven" (1.1.9–10).

The young lovers perfectly reproduce the conventional idealizing imagery of the period.

O Helen, goddess, nymph, perfect, divine!
To what, my love, shall I compare thine eyne?
Crystal is muddy. O, how ripe in show
Thy lips, those kissing cherries, tempting grow!
That pure congealèd white, high Taurus' snow,
Fanned with the eastern wind, turns to a crow
When thou hold'st up thy hand.

                                                      (3.2.140–46)

Eyes like crystals, lips like cherries, hands white as snow—
this is engaging to the degree that it is lyrical. It is also delightfully absurd, when we bear in mind that it is the instant
effect of Robin Goodfellow's love-juice, and represents a vision of Helena that Demetrius was quite unable to see before
his sight was bewitched. But as Helena herself explains earlier in the play, love does not necessarily see what is there:

Thing base and vile, holding no quantity,
Love can transpose to form and dignity.

MARRIAGE BASED ON MUTUAL LOVE

*Upper class marriage in the Middle Ages was often based
on economic or political factors, and it was under the control of fathers. By Shakespeare's day, however, a new view of
marriage was in the ascendancy, a view that stressed companionship, mutual love, and the choice of partners. As Egeus, the
father of Hermia, demonstrates in* A Midsummer Night's
Dream, *the power and concern of fathers could still be formidable. In this play, as scholar Helen Hackett observes, a happy
harmony is achieved between the lovers' choice of partners and
the patriarchal social order.*

Part of the sense of happiness at this play's ending is created by
its participation in the relatively new ideology that marriage
should be predominantly based on love. This is not the place to
give a comprehensive history of attitudes to marriage, but in very
general terms sixteenth- and seventeenth-century marriage-
theory can be contrasted with that of the Middle Ages. In the earlier period, upper-class marriages were usually dynastic alliances
rather than love-matches, and literary culture tended to locate
passion outside marriage in what has been called 'courtly love' or
'fin amour', the devotion of a lover who self-deprecatingly styled
himself as servant to his married mistress. Meanwhile, the
Catholic Church emphatically advocated virginity, especially female virginity, as a higher state of virtue than matrimony. The
Reformation brought shifts in these ideologies: marriage began to
be prized as a means of preventing sexual irregularity and as a

Love looks not with the eyes but with the mind;
And therefore is winged Cupid painted blind.

(1.1.238–41)

Helena's words might equally constitute a commentary on
Titania's first response to Bottom braying in his ass's head:
"What angel wakes me from my flow'ry bed?" (3.1.131). The
fairy queen's temporary devotion to a donkey is the play's
clearest and funniest indication of love's arbitrary nature.

One reason why the lovers seem comic is that their
changes of preference do not appear arbitrary to them. As
Lysander solemnly explains to his new love, Helena, "The
will of man is by his reason swayed, / And reason says you
are the worthier maid" (2.2.122–23). The element of absurdity is compounded when we recognize (though they do not)
a parody of their idealizing vision in Thisbe's lament for the
dead Pyramus:

virtuous state in its own right; this in turn meant that marriage
had to be what has been termed 'companionate', based on the
contended monogamy of each partner; and this in turn meant
that marriage needed to be based on mutual love. Enforced marriage was increasingly seen as a greater threat to the stability of
family and society than clandestine marriage for love: thus a
writer addressing 'the Gentlewomen and others of England' in
1593 asked, rhetorically, 'What is the cause of so many household breaches, divorcements, and continual discontentments, but
unnatural disagreements by unmutual contracts?'

A number of recent discussions of sixteenth- and seventeenth-
century marriage have concluded that, although companionate
marriage allowed some degrees of autonomy to women, these re-
mained within restricted limits. It created a social structure in
which in theory '[m]arriage is an equal partnership', but in practice
'some partners are more equal than others' [as scholar Lisa Jardine
comments]. As we have seen, in *A Midsummer Night's Dream* the
final marriages are achieved through patriarchal means and on
patriarchal terms; not only does Jack have Jill, but, as Puck goes on
to sing, 'The man shall have his mare again, / And all shall be well'
(III.ii. 463–4). Nevertheless, the final scenes show a fortunate coin-
cidence of free choice in love, including female choice, with the patriarchal social order. The strength of patriarchal matrimony is
most powerfully reinforced if it is something to which the potentially wayward and wilful female *voluntarily* submits.

Helen Hackett, *A Midsummer Night's Dream*. Plymouth, UK: Northcote House,
1997, pp. 32–33.

> These lily lips
> This cherry nose,
> These yellow cowslip cheeks
> Are gone, are gone!
> Lovers, make moan;
> His eyes were green as leeks.
>   (5.1.347–52)

The king and queen of the fairies are old (or, rather, age-less) married lovers, and they are quarreling. The play does not ignore the trace of violence that exists within love when the other person fails to conform to the lover's idealized image. The quarrel between Oberon and Titania has upset the proper sequence of the seasons, which is a serious problem in a society based on agriculture, though it is hard for the audience to feel great anxiety about this when the fairies quarrel so musically:

> These are the forgeries of jealousy;
> And never, since the middle summer's spring,
> Met we on hill, in dale, forest, or mead,
> By pavèd fountain or by rushy brook,
> Or in the beachèd margent of the sea,
> To dance our ringlets to the whistling wind,
> But with thy brawls thou hast disturbed our sport.
>   (2.1.84–90)

The brawls are not mentioned until the verse has quite distracted us from the substance of the quarrel through its evocation of imaginary landscapes, so lacking in specific detail that they seem the settings of half-remembered legends and tales of adventure. No wonder Oberon and Titania are finally reconciled. In a similar way, lyricism and comedy distance the passionate quarrels between Demetrius and Lysander, Hermia and Helena. Conversely, if the play of "Pyramus and Thisbe" evokes tears of laughter rather than sorrow (5.1.73–74), it alludes, nevertheless, to the tragic possibilities of a conflict between love and parental opposition. *A Midsummer Night's Dream* does not let its audience forget that love entails confusion and danger as well as grace, although it never entirely separates these contraries.

The Elusive Nature of Love

None of the distinct voices in the play—romantic, lyrical, or urgent—seems to exhaust the character of love; none of them can be identified with "true" love as opposed to false. Nor does any of them summarize the nature of love; and when Theseus tries to do so, what he says seems quite inadequate. "I never may be-

lieve," he insists, "These antique fables, nor these fairy toys"
(5.1.2–3). "Antique" implies both "ancient" and "antic" (theatrical), and ironically Theseus himself is both. He is a fictional
hero of classical legend and a figure on a stage in the most theatrical of plays. As for the fairy stories he repudiates, we have
seen them enacted in the course of the play, and we are therefore in no position to share his entirely rational dismissal of
lovers, along with lunatics and poets (5.1.7). Hippolyta seems
more to the point when she answers him, but she is consider-
ably less than specific. The separate stories of the night, she affirms, grow "to something of great constancy [consistency], /
But, howsoever, strange and admirable [eliciting wonder]"
(5.1.27–28). In talking about love, as perhaps in love itself, there
is commonly a sense of a quality that cannot be made present,
cannot be presented, or represented. In the most exhaustive
analysis, the most effusive declaration, or the most lyrical
poem, something slips away, and it is that elusiveness that sus-
tains desire itself, as well as the desire to talk about it.

And this, perhaps, is a clue to the nature of the pleasure *A
Midsummer Night's Dream* offers its audience. It constructs for
the spectators something of the desire it also puts on display. In
one sense comedy produces the wishes it then goes on to ful-
fill. The play invites us to sympathize with the young lovers. In
consequence, we want Hermia to marry the man she loves, in
spite of the opposition of her ridiculous father, who supposes
that serenades and love tokens are forms of witchcraft. And we
want Helena to be happy with Demetrius in spite of his initial
rejection of her love. The enigma that enlists the desire of the
audience centers on whether the play will bring about the
happy ending we hope for, and if so, how. The pleasure of this
dramatic form is familiar from Roman comedy to Neil Simon,
and its familiarity is precisely part of the enjoyment we are invited to experience.

But *A Midsummer Night's Dream* does not always do exactly
what we might expect, and in this way it keeps its audience
guessing, continually reoffering itself in the process as an object of our desire. The play begins with the longing of Theseus
and Hippolyta to consummate their love, and the action that follows occupies the intervening space, so that at the end of Act 5
the newly married lovers go off to bed together. Desire constitutes the frame of the play itself. In the meantime, Theseus dis-
patches the master of the revels, who is responsible for entertainment at court, in search of "merriments" and "reveling"

(1.1.13, 20), and at once an old man comes in with his daughter and her two rival suitors. Egeus is appropriately stagy ("Stand forth, Demetrius . . . Stand forth, Lysander" [1.1.25, 27]), and the audience might be expected to recognize the pattern of Roman comedy, familiar from the plays of Plautus and Terence and widely imitated in Elizabethan drama. The conventional poetry and the extravagance of the lovers intensifies the sense that we are watching the first of the revels that Theseus has sent for, a play within a play.

But Roman comedy does not characteristically include fairies, and it is the mischief-making Robin Goodfellow, a supernatural figure from English folklore, who largely motivates the plot of this inset play. The genres are mixed, with the effect that the audience is never quite sure whether the conventions in operation at any specific moment are those of comedy or folktale. At the same time, Robin Goodfellow (Puck) both is and is not a native English replica of the blind, irrational, overhasty, and Continental Cupid that Helena describes. The play teases the audience with glimpses of familiar forms and figures, and then deflects our attention onto something unexpected. In consequence, the delight it invites the spectators to experience is entirely distinct from the comfortable feeling of recognition other plays rely on.

THE RESOLUTION OF THE PLAY

The plot leads up to the marriages of the lovers, but it does not quite confirm the distinction we might expect it to identify between true love on the one hand and arbitrary passion induced by magic on the other. Demetrius still has the love-juice on his eyes, and yet the play gives no indication of a difference between this marriage and the others. If marriage is a serious social institution, it seems to rest on a remarkably precarious base. But the imperatives of fiction require that the comedy of love end in marriage, and Demetrius marries the partner he has when the action comes to a stop.

If the story leads up to marriage, however, it does not quite end there. Many critical accounts of the play depend on an opposition between its two locations, the house of Theseus in Athens and the wildwood under the control of the fairies. The Athenian court represents the world of reconciliation and rationality, of social institutions and communal order, while the wood outside Athens is the location of night and bewildering passions, a place of anarchy and anxiety, where behavior becomes unpredictable and individual identity is transformed. On this reading, the fairies, who are by no means the sugary creatures of Victorian fantasy, represent the quintessence of all that is turbulent and uncontrolled in human experience, and in particular the traces of instability and violence that inhabit desire.

At the end of the play, however, when the couples, now properly distributed and legitimately married, have gone to bed, the fairies come in from the wood and take possession of the palace: "Through the house give glimmering light, / By the dead and drowsy fire . . ." (5.1.408–9). Though their purpose, we are to understand, is benevolent, they also bring with them the uncanny resonances of the dreamworld that seemed to have been left behind in the wood:

> . . . we fairies, that do run
> By the triple Hecate's team
> From the presence of the sun,
> Following darkness like a dream
> Now are frolic.
>
> (5.1.400–4)

Hecate is the queen of the night, and the team the fairies run with are the dragons who draw her chariot. Their unexpected presence within the house, therefore, implies the invasion of elements of the turbulent, the magical, and the unearthly into the social and domestic proprieties of marriage.

How could it be otherwise? This is, after all, a wedding night. But by handing over the conclusion to the fairies, the play displaces the apparent closure, the celebration of restored identity and the return to community it has duly delivered. Instead, it goes on to re-create what is most mysterious and elusive in the world it has portrayed, and gives the stage back to the representatives of all that is unaccountable and still unrecounted in the experience of love. In this way *A Midsummer Night's Dream* offers to leave its audience in a state of mind that bears some resemblance to Bottom's when he wakes up from *his* dream: exalted, perhaps, but a little less assured, less confident, and altogether less knowing than before.

The Lovers' Transformation

Alexander Leggatt

In the view of scholar Alexander Leggatt of the University of Toronto, each of the four groups of characters in *A Midsummer Night's Dream* is subject to its own kind of folly, but each keeps its own integrity as well. In this respect, the play continually reminds us of the limitations of perception as we see the narrow perspective each set of characters brings to the experiences of others. Bottom in the arms of Titania, Egeus confronted with Hermia's romantic attachment—all the characters suffer from limited perspective. The four young lovers are themselves subject to passionate and irrational choices based on their narrow perspective. Yet their folly is tempered by the presence of Oberon and Puck, who serve to remind us that the lovers are under the sway of a power greater than themselves. According to Leggatt, their purely subjective behavior, though lacking in self-awareness, has a coherence and an integrity to it as well.

When Titania meets Bottom in the wood near Athens, we see a fairy confronting a mortal, and finding him more wonderful than he finds her. For Titania, Bottom—ass's head and all —is an object of rare grace and beauty; for Bottom, the queen of the fairies is a lady he has just met, who is behaving a bit strangely, but who can be engaged in ordinary, natural conversation:

> TITANIA: I pray thee, gentle mortal, sing again.
> Mine ear is much enamoured of thy note;
> So is mine eye enthralled to thy shape;
> And thy fair virtue's force perforce doth move me,
> On the first view, to say, to swear, I love thee.
> BOTTOM: Methinks, mistress, you should have little reason
> for that. And yet, to say the truth, reason and love
> keep little company together now-a-days. The

> more the pity that some honest neighbours will
> not make them friends. Nay, I can gleek upon oc-
> casion.

TITANIA: Thou art as wise as thou art beautiful.

(III. i. 125–35)

This is, by now, a familiar effect. Behind the sharply contrasted voices are two utterly different kinds of understanding, and each one comically dislocates the other. Titania's
love is addressed to a hearer who uses it simply as the occasion for a bit of cheerful philosophizing. And the philosophy,
in turn, is wasted on the listener. It is all very well for Bottom to chatter away about reason and love; he has the detachment of the totally immune. But Titania is caught up in
the experience of which Bottom is only a detached observer,
and, ironically, his cool philosophy only gives her one more
reason for adoring him. . . .

Bottom and Titania present the play's most striking image, a pairing of disparate beings whose contact only emphasizes the difference between them. It looks for a moment
as though the barrier between the mortal and immortal
worlds has fallen; but on inspection, the barrier proves as
secure as ever. Instead of a fusion of worlds we are given a
series of neat comic contrasts. And throughout the play, we
see four different groups of characters—the lovers, the
clowns, the older Athenians and the fairies—each group
preoccupied with its own limited problems, and largely unaware of the others. When they make contact, it is usually to
emphasize the difference between them. All are to some degree innocent, though (as we shall see) the degree of innocence varies. But the play weaves them all together. Each
group, so self-absorbed, is seen in a larger context, which
provides comic perspective. Each in turn provides a similar
context for the others, and if here and there we feel tempted
to take sides, we can never do so for very long; for while
each group has its own folly, it has its own integrity as well,
and its own special, coherent view of life.

We are reminded throughout of the workings of perception,
and in particular of the way we depend on perception—
special and limited though it may be—for our awareness of
the world. When Hermia finds Lysander, who has run away
from her, her first words appear to be a digression:

> Dark night, that from the eye his function takes,
> The ear more quick of apprehension makes;
> Wherein it doth impair the seeing sense,

It pays the hearing double recompense.
Thou art not by mine eye, Lysander, found;
Mine ear, I thank it, brought me to thy sound.

(III. ii. 177–82)

The natural question—'But why unkindly didst thou leave
me so?'—is asked only after she has discoursed in general
terms on how the senses work. In the clown scenes, there is
a recurring joke by which the senses are comically trans-
posed (III. i. 81–2; IV. i. 206–9; V. i. 190–1). For the most part,
however, the general point is absorbed into the particular
dramatic situations of the play. The conflict between Hermia
and her father, for example, is seen as a difference of perception:

HERMIA: I would my father look'd but with my eyes.
THESEUS: Rather your eyes must with his judgement look.

(I. i. 56–7)

When Hermia and Egeus look at Lysander, they see two different people, for she sees with the eyes of love, he with the
eyes of cantankerous old age, obsessed with its own authority.

THE FORCE AND INTEGRITY OF LOVE

In the opening scene, the lovers are on the defensive, set
against the hostility of Egeus and the more restrained, re-
gretful opposition of Theseus. Egeus's lecture to Lysander
presents love from an outsider's point of view, as trivial, de-
ceitful and disruptive of good order:

Thou hast by moon light at her window sung,
With feigning voice, verses of feigning love,
And stol'n the impression of her fantasy
With bracelets of thy hair, rings, gawds, conceits,
Knacks, trifles, nosegays, sweetmeats, messengers
Of strong prevailment in unhardened youth;
With cunning hast thou filch'd my daughter's heart;
Turn'd her obedience, which is due to me,
To stubborn harshness.

(I. i. 30–8)

Against this crabbed but concrete and detailed attack, Hermia's defence, though deeply felt, is inarticulate: 'I know not
by what power I am made bold . . .' (I. i. 59). But it suggests
that love is a force bearing down all normal authority, and
arming the lover with strength to meet the hostility of the
outside world. It gives Hermia the courage to defy her father
and the Duke in open court, and to accept the pains and
trials love must always bear:

If then true lovers have been ever cross'd,
It stands as an edict in destiny.
Then let us teach our trial patience,
Because it is a customary cross . . .

(I. i. 150–3)

Love, to the outsider, appears foolish; but in accepting its demands the lovers acquire their own kind of integrity. Their vision of the world is transformed. In Hermia's words,

Before the time I did Lysander see,
Seem'd Athens as a paradise to me.
O, then, what graces in my love do dwell,
That he hath turn'd a heaven into a hell!

(I. i. 204–7)

And for Helena the forest is similarly transformed by the presence of Demetrius:

It is not night when I do see your face,
Therefore I think I am not in the night,
Nor doth this wood lack worlds of company,
For you, in my respect, are all the world.

(II. i. 221–4)

But there is also something comically irrational in these transformations. In particular, the lover's perception of his beloved, and his judgement of her, are peculiar and inexplicable, so much so that even to the lovers themselves love seems blind. As Hermia says of Demetrius,

And as he errs, doting on Hermia's eyes,
So I, admiring of his qualities.
Things base and vile, holding no quantity,
Love can transpose to form and dignity.
Love looks not with the eyes, but with the mind;
And therefore is wing'd Cupid painted blind.
Nor hath Love's mind of any judgment taste;
Wings and no eyes figure unheedy haste;
And therefore is Love said to be a child,
Because in choice he is so oft beguil'd.

(I. i. 239–9)

It is not Hermia's beauty that inspires Demetrius's love: 'Through Athens I am thought as fair as she' (I. i. 227). It is rather that love imposes its own peculiar kind of vision, which renders any other opinion—including that of common sense—irrelevant. How far Helena's own senses have been taken over by this vision may be judged by her decision to betray her friend to Demetrius:

for this intelligence
If I have thanks, it is a dear expense.

But herein mean I to enrich my pain,
To have his sight thither and back again.   (I. i. 248–51)

In love, the mere sight of the beloved acquires an importance that by any normal standards would be absurd.

CONVENTIONAL EXPRESSIONS OF LOVE

The lovers may find each other's choices inexplicable, but at least they share the same kind of experience: they are in the grip of a power that renders choice and will meaningless. One sign of this is that the lovers lack the conscious awareness of convention that distinguishes Berowne and the ladies in *Love's Labour's Lost*. They slip naturally into a stylized manner of speech:

LYSANDER:	Ay me! For aught that I could ever read,
	Could ever learn by tale or history,
	The course of true love never did run smooth;
	But either it was different in blood—
HERMIA:	O cross! too high to be enthrall'd to low.
LYSANDER:	Or else ingraffed in respect of years—
HERMIA:	O spite! too old to be engag'd to young.
LYSANDER:	Or else it stood upon the choice of friends—
HERMIA:	O hell! to choose love by another's eyes.

(I. i. 132–40)

There is something ceremonial about this passage, with its liturgical responses, and like all ceremonies it presents the individual experience as part of a larger and more general pattern. The individual can assert his independence of this process only by showing his awareness of it and standing partly outside it, as Berowne attempts to do. But Lysander and Hermia surrender to the ceremony, taking its patterned language as a normal mode of speech. Later in the same scene, Hermia falls into a playful, teasing style as she swears to meet Lysander:

I swear to thee by Cupid's strongest bow,
By his best arrow with the golden head,
By the simplicity of Venus' doves,
By that which knitteth souls and prospers loves,
And by that fire which burn'd the Carthage Queen,
When the false Troyan under sail was seen,
By all the vows that ever men have broke,
In number more than ever women spoke,
In that same place thou hast appointed me,
Tomorrow truly will I meet with thee.

(I. i. 169–78)

There is, this time, a deliberate playfulness in the way the literary allusions pile up, as she teases her lover by comparing male infidelity and female faith. But the speech flows swiftly and easily, and the joking does no damage; she can afford to toy with her love because she is so sure of it. (There is a similar quality in their affectionate banter about sleeping arrangements in the forest—II. ii. 39–61.) The joking with love is not that of an outsider exposing its weakness, but that of an insider confident of its strength, and feeling that strength by subjecting it to a little harmless teasing. And once again, the character herself gives no indication that this manner of speech is anything other than perfectly natural.

The exchange on the course of true love is slow and brooding; Hermia's speech, swift and gay. The common factor is an air of literary artifice that sets the lovers' experience apart as something special; and throughout the play the range of expression achieved within this framework of artifice is remarkable. We see this, for example, when Lysander awakes to find himself in love with Helena:

> The will of man is by his reasons sway'd,
> And reason says you are the worthier maid.
> Things growing are not ripe until their season;
> So I, being young, till now ripe not to reason;
> And touching now the point of human skill,
> Reason becomes the marshal to my will,
> And leads me to your eyes, where I o'erlook
> Love's stories, written in Love's richest book.

HELENA: Wherefore was I to this keen mockery born?
> When at your hands did I deserve this scorn?
> Is't not enough, is't not enough, young man,
> That I did never, no, nor never can,
> Deserve a sweet look from Demetrius' eye,
> But you must flout my insufficiency?
> Good troth, you do me wrong, good sooth, you do,
> In such disdainful manner me to woo.

(II. ii. 115–30)

Lysander's speech is formal, solemn, sententious—and thoroughly dislocated by its context. He describes his love as natural and reasonable, but we know it is purely arbitrary. Here the character's unawareness of his own dependence on convention becomes sharply comic. Helena's irritable retort gives us, by contrast, the sound of a natural speaking voice; there is a striking difference in tone and pace. And yet it too is in rhyming couplets: her seemingly natural utterance is still contained within the framework of a convention; her anger, no less than his infatuation, is part of the larger, dance-like pattern in which all four lovers are unconsciously moving.

THE AUDIENCE'S IRONIC DETACHMENT

The lovers see their experiences in the forest as chaotic; but for the audience the disorder, like the disorder of a Feydeau farce, is neatly organized, giving us pleasure where it gives them pain. When Hermia accuses Demetrius of killing Lysander, the patterned language and the rhymed couplets cool the emotional impact the scene might have had (III. ii. 43–81). Over and over, the violence of the ideas is lightened by jingling rhythm and rhyme: 'I'll follow thee, and make a heaven of hell, / To die upon the hand I love so well' (II. i. 243–4). It is not so much that, as Enid Welsford suggests, 'the harmony and grace of the action would have been spoilt by convincing passion'; it is more that the manner of the action in itself ensures that the passion is convincing only to the characters. They lash out frantically at each other, but the audience is too far away to share in their feelings. Our detachment is aided by the presence of Puck and Oberon, acting as an onstage audience and providing a comic perspective. What is serious and painful to the lovers is simply a 'fond pageant' of mortal foolishness to the watchers (III. ii. 144). Puck in particular regards the whole affair as a show put on for his amusement (and incidentally if we can remember this in the final scene it adds a level of irony to the lovers' laughter as they watch Pyramus and Thisbe: they too, not so long ago, amused an audience with antics that they thought were serious). The irony is compounded when the lovers indignantly accuse each other of playing games with serious feelings: 'Wink at each other; hold the sweet jest up; / This sport, well carried, shall be chronicled' (III. ii. 239–40). Helena's accusation is very close to the truth—except that it should be directed at the audience.

But our feelings are subtly managed here: there are two watchers—Puck, with his delight in chaos, and Oberon, who wishes to bring chaos to an end. We share in both these attitudes. When Helena recalls her childhood friendship with Hermia, the rhyme slips away and it becomes a little easier to take the characters' feelings seriously (III. ii. 195–219). From this point on, the formality breaks down into undignified, farcical squabbling, with physical knockabout and coarse insults—relieved, on one occasion, by a surprisingly quiet and dignified speech from Helena:

> Good Hermia, do not be so bitter with me.
> I evermore did love you, Hermia,
> Did ever keep your counsel, never wrong'd you;
> Save that, in love unto Demetrius,
> I told him of your stealth unto this wood. . . .
> And now, so you will let me quiet go,
> To Athens I will bear my folly back,
> And follow you no further.
>
> (III. ii. 306–16)

While still enjoying the confusion, we are beginning to feel that it had better stop soon. And Oberon and Puck see that it does.

But we are kept at a distance from the lovers' final union, no less than from their suffering. In the last stages of their ordeal, formality returns and is further heightened: a variety of rhymed verse forms accumulates as, one by one, the lovers enter and fall asleep. Their individuality is at a particularly low ebb, as Puck controls them more directly than ever, even to the point of assuming the men's voices (III. ii. 396–463). The final harmony he creates for them, like the earlier confusion, is seen as the working out of a dance pattern; and more than that, it is the fulfilment of a ritual sense of life, embodied in homely clichés:

> And the country proverb known,
> That every man should take his own,
> In your waking shall be shown.
> > Jack shall have Jill;
> > Nought shall go ill;
> The man shall have is mare again, and all shall be well.
>
> (III. ii. 458–63)

Similarly, Theseus sees their coupling in terms of sport and pastime—'No doubt they rose up early to observe / The rite of May' (IV. i. 129–30)—and as a fulfilment of nature's most basic impulse: 'Good morrow, friends. Saint Valentine is past; / Begin these wood-birds but to couple now?' (IV. i. 136–7). The presence, and the comments, of other characters provide the awareness of convention that the lovers themselves lack, being too caught up in their own experiences. We see love's perceptions as special and limited, and the lovers themselves as lacking in full self-awareness. The magic flower is applied, significantly, to the eye; just as significantly, it is applied while the lover is asleep. And even the final harmony of love, when seen through the homely analogies of Puck and Theseus, is satisfying but nothing to get ecstatic about: 'The man shall have his mare again, and all shall be well' sounds like the voice of a parent comforting a child who has been making a great fuss about nothing. It is certainly not how the lovers themselves would have put it. At the same time, however, we recognize that the lovers *have* got what they want: the law of Athens, so formidable in the first scene, is swept away to accommodate them, and Egeus is reduced to spluttering impotence. In our final attitude to the lovers, there is respect as well as amused detachment.

The Dark Side of Love and Marriage

David Bevington

Over the past thirty years, many productions of *A Midsummer Night's Dream* have chosen to emphasize the potential violence of the woods, the malevolence of the fairies, and the unrepressed sexuality lurking beneath the surface of the play. In this interpretation of the play, love is a dangerous and painful preoccupation, and sexuality is animalistic, never far from rape and other usually repressed desires. Noted scholar David Bevington of the University of Chicago concedes that there is a dark and threatening element in the play's depiction of desire and love and marriage, yet he argues that this dimension of the play is counterbalanced by persistent comic reassurance. The tension between these tendencies in the play is exemplified by the presence of Puck and Oberon, who represent contrasting forces in the fairy kingdom.

When Oberon instructs Puck, in act 3, scene 2 of *A Midsummer Night's Dream*, to overcast the night with "drooping fog as black as Acheron," and to lead the "testy rivals" Demetrius and Lysander astray so that they will not actually harm one another in their rivalry, while Oberon for his part undertakes to obtain the changeling boy from Titania whom he will then release from her infatuated love of Bottom, Puck replies that the two of them will have to work fast. Such fairy doings need to be accomplished by night, insists Puck. With the approaching break of day, and the shining of Aurora's harbinger or morning star, ghosts and damned spirits will have to trip home to churchyards and their "wormy beds" beneath the ground. Puck's implication seems clear: he and Oberon, being spirits of the dark, are bound by its rules to avoid the light of day.

Just as clearly, however, Oberon protests that Puck is wrong in making such an assumption. "But we are spirits of another sort," Oberon insists.

> I with the Morning's love have oft made sport,
> And, like a forester, the groves may tread
> Even till the eastern gate, all fiery red,
> Opening on Neptune, with fair blessèd beams
> Turns into yellow gold his salt green streams.
>
> [3.2. 388–93]

Oberon may frolic until late in the dawn, though by implication even he may not stay abroad all day. The association of Oberon with sunlight and dawn is thus more symbolic than practical; it disassociates him from spirits of the dark, even though he must finish up this night's work before night is entirely past. He concedes to Puck the need for hurry: "But notwithstanding, haste; make no delay. / We may effect this business yet ere day." The concession implies that Oberon has made his point about sporting with the dawn not to refute Puck's call for swiftness, but to refute Puck's association of the fairies with ghosts and damned spirits.

This debate between Oberon and Puck reflects a fundamental tension in the play between comic reassurance and the suggestion of something dark and threatening. Although the fairies act benignly, Puck continually hints at a good deal more than simple mischief. The forest itself is potentially a place of violent death and rape, even if the lovers experience nothing more than fatigue, anxiety, and being torn by briars. In the forest, moreover, the experience of love invites all lovers to consider, however briefly, the opportunity for sexual reveling freed from the restraints of social custom. Of late, Jan Kott has shown to us most forcefully this dark side of love; indeed, he has done so too forcefully, and with an often exaggerated effect upon contemporary productions of this and other plays. Still, his insight has something to commend it. . . . Even today, we find it distasteful to speak openly of sexual longing in this comedy, for fear of dealing grossly with the play's delicately understated portrayal of Eros. My purpose, however, is to suggest that in its proper context the dark side of love is seldom very far away in this play.

Order and Disorder in Fairyland

Let us return to the debate between Oberon and Puck, and to Shakespeare's dramatic purpose in presenting to us both the king of fairies and his mischievous attendant. This purpose is not restricted to the fairies' function in the plot, in which Puck comically misapplies Oberon's ambiguous instructions about the love juice or extemporaneously creates a monster with whom Titania is to fall in love. Puck constantly brings before our eyes a more threatening vision of fairydom than is apparent in Oberon's more regal pronouncements. In part, of course, he is the practical joker making Oberon laugh at his ability to mimic a filly foal, or a three-foot stool, or Demetrius and Lysander. Puck is infinitely versatile in changing shapes, just as he can also put a girdle round the earth in forty minutes. On the other hand, Puck also loves to frighten people. He gladly confesses to being the elf who "frights the maidens of the villagery" (2.1.35). It is he who conjures up, for the delectation of the audience, a morbid image of nighttime as fearful, and as associated with gaping graves in churchyards, ghosts and damned spirits, screeching owls, and howling wolves:

> Now the hungry lion roars,
> And the wolf behowls the moon;
> Whilst the heavy ploughman snores,
> All with weary task fordone.
> Now the wasted brands do glow,
> Whilst the screech owl, screeching loud,
> Puts the wretch that lies in woe
> In remembrance of a shroud.
> Now it is the time of night
> That the graves, all gaping wide,
> Every one lets forth his sprite,
> In the churchyard paths to glide.
>
> [5.1.360–71]

Although, as he says, the fairies are now "frolic," their usual custom is to run "By the triple Hecate's team / From the presence of the sun." Earlier, too, as we have seen, Puck associates his own nocturnal activities with "night's swift dragons" and with ghosts "wand'ring here and there," "damnèd spirits all, / That in crossways and floods have burial," hastening home to their "wormy beds" before the break of day, lest the daylight should "look their shames upon" (3.2.379–85).

Even in the action of the play, Puck does in fact frighten many of the persons he meets—virtually all of them, in fact, except Bottom. As he chases Quince, Snout, and the rest from their rehearsal spot in a forest clearing, he makes the incantation:

I'll follow you; I'll lead you about a round,
Through bog, through bush, through brake, through brier.
Sometime a horse I'll be, sometime a hound,
A hog, a headless bear, sometime a fire;
And neigh, and bark, and grunt, and roar, and burn,
Like horse, hound, hog, bear, fire, at every turn.
[3.1.96–101]

And he later reports to his master, with glee, the startling effect upon the rude mechanicals created by Bottom's reemergence from his hawthorne tiring house with an ass's head on his shoulders:

When they him spy,
As wild geese that the creeping fowler eye,
Or russet-pated choughs, many in sort,
Rising and cawing at the gun's report,
Sever themselves and madly sweep the sky;
So at his sight away his fellows fly,
And at our stamp here o'er and o'er one falls;
He murder cries and help from Athens calls.
Their sense thus weak, lost with their fears thus strong,
Made senseless things begin to do them wrong,
For briers and thorns at their apparel snatch:
Some, sleeves—some, hats; from yielders all things catch.
[3.2.19–30]

Our own laughter at this comic chase should not obscure the fact that Puck creates truly frightening illusions in the forest. Similarly, our sense of assurance that Demetrius and Lysander will come to no harm must not cause us to forget that Puck's game with them is to lead them astray, like those night-wanderers whom he is known to mislead, "laughing at their harm" (2.1.39).

In the relationship of Puck and Oberon, it is Puck who tends to stress the irrational and frightening while Oberon's position is that of a ruler insisting on the establishment of proper obedience to his authority. When Puck mistakenly applies the love-juice intended for Demetrius to Lysander's eyes, thereby inducing Lysander to desert his true love for Helena, Oberon's first reaction is one of dismay:

What hast thou done? Thou hast mistaken quite
And laid the love-juice on some true-love's sight.
Of thy misprison must perforce ensue
Some true-love turned, and not a false turned true.
[3.2.88–91]

Whereupon the fairy king immediately orders Puck to find Helena and return with her, so that Demetrius (who now lies asleep at their feet) can be induced to love her. Oberon seeks always to right unhappy love. His insistence that he and his followers are fairies of "another sort" is thus an appropriate and consistent stance for him, even if what he says does not always square with Puck's role as the hobgoblin who skims milk of its cream, prevents milk from turning into butter, or deprives ale of its "barm" or head. Oberon's very presence at the wedding is intended to assure that such things won't happen to Theseus, Hippolyta, and the rest of the happy young people about to marry; Oberon guarantees that their issue "Ever shall be fortunate," free of "mole, harelip, nor scar," or any other "blots of Nature's hand" (5.1.395–400).

Together, Oberon and Puck represent contrasting forces within the fairy kingdom. Perhaps their functions can best be reconciled by reflecting that their chief power to do good lies in withholding the mischief of which they are capable. Like Apollo in book 1 of the *Iliad*, whom the Greek warriors venerate as the god of health because he is also terrifyingly capable of sending plagues, Oberon is to be feared because he has the authority both to prevent birth defects and other marks "Prodigious, such as are / Despisèd in nativity" (5.1.401–2), and to inflict them. Only when placated by men and called by such names as Hobgoblin or "sweet Puck" will these spirits work for men and bring them good luck.

THE AMBIVALENT FOREST

The forest shares many of these same ambivalent qualities as do the fairies. It is in part a refuge for young lovers fleeing the sharp Athenian law, a convenient and secluded spot for clandestine play rehearsals, and a fragrant bower for the fairy queen decked out "With sweet musk-roses, and with eglantine" (2.1.252). For the young lovers, however, as their quest for amorous bliss grows more and more vexed, the forest becomes increasingly a place of darkness, estrangement, and potential violence. Demetrius warns Helena, in an attempt to be rid of her,

> You do impeach your modesty too much
> To leave the city and commit yourself
> Into the hands of one that loves you not,
> To trust the opportunity of night
> And the ill counsel on a desert place
> With the rich worth of your virginity.
>
> [2.1.214–19]

Demetrius recognizes the opportunity for a loveless rape and briefly recognizes his own potential for such sexual violence, though he is also virtuous enough to reject the temptation. The alternative he offers Helena is scarcely more kind: he will run from her and leave her "to the mercy of wild beasts" (l. 228).

The ever-present moon shares this same ambivalence. Although it is at times the beneficent moon shining at its full on the palace wood to facilitate a rehearsal (1.2) or through a casement window of the great chamber where the final performance of "Pyramus and Thisbe" is to take place (3.1), it is contrastingly an old waning moon, associated with age and inhibition of pleasures, lingering the desires of would-be lovers "Like to a stepdame or a dowager, / Long withering out a young man's revenue" (1.1.6–7). More ominously, the moon is "the governess of floods," who "Pale in her anger, washes all the air, / That rheumatic diseases do abound" (2.1.103–5), whenever the fairy king and queen are at enmity. Even if the "chaste beams of the wat'ry moon" call up associations of that "fair vestal," Queen Elizabeth (2.1.158–64), and seem to offer assurances of the kind of di-

---

ROMANTIC LOVE AND APPETITE

For scholars such as Peter Hyland, the romantic love on view in A Midsummer Night's Dream *is troublesome. It is, above all, arbitrary and irrational, based on fantasy. Romantic love in the play is consistently compromised by the presence of appetite, as evidenced by Theseus' conquering of Hippolyta and by Oberon's willingness to humiliate and dominate Titania.*

A Midsummer Night's Dream is Shakespeare's most complex and most comprehensive account of romantic illusion. Love is seen, in effect, as fantasy, an inexplicable and irrational preference. In the opening scene there is a division between Hermia, who wishes to marry Lysander, and her father Egeus, who wishes her to marry Demetrius, which precipitates a move out from the oppressive court world to the healing green world of the forest. Egeus's demand seems arbitrary given that, as Lysander says, the two young men are alike in most things (1.1.99–102); however, the play shows that the choices of love are also arbitrary, a matter of 'dotage'. The irrationality of love is represented by the actions of the fairies, particularly Puck, whose manipulation of the affections of the four young lovers from one object to another suggests that love has no grounding in anything real. When the lovers are

vine protection afforded the young lady in Milton's *Comus,* the moon is not permitted to shine continually throughout the nighttime misadventures of this play. Oberon orders Puck, as we have seen, to overcast the night. "The starry welkin cover thou anon / With drooping fog as black as Acheron" (3.2.355–57). In the ensuing darkness, the lovers stress repeatedly their sense of bewilderment and discouragement. "O weary night, O long and tedious night," complains Helena, "Abate thy hours" (3.2.431–32,). The word "weary" sounds a choric note of repetition in Hermia's entrance, immediately following the speech just quoted: "Never so weary, never so in woe, / Bedabbled with the dew, and torn with briers, / I can no further crawl" (ll. 442–44). Lysander, having fallen as he says "in dark uneven way," has already given up pursuit of Demetrius, who all unawares joins his archrival "on this cold bed" (ll. 417, 429). Although the lovers are together, and although their tribulations are now at an end, the nighttime experience has been one of separation, humiliation, and defeat. As Puck observes ear-

restored to one another at the end of the play it is poetically but uneasily satisfying.

The unease comes from a sense that behind the apparent selflessness of romantic love there lies only appetite, the desire to impose one's own needs upon the object of love. This appears to be the case with Oberon and Titania, the play's married couple. Their quarrel over the changeling boy is explosive enough to cause disorder in nature, and there is something ugly and violent in Oberon's willingness to humiliate his wife in order to get his way. This violence echoes that of Theseus in his winning of Hippolyta: 'I woo'd thee with my sword, / And won thy love doing thee injuries' (1.1.16–17), he says to her, and indeed Theseus's history of relationships with women is a history of violence and betrayal, as indicated by Oberon:

> Didst thou not lead him through the glimmering night
> From Perigouna, whom he ravished,
> And make him with fair Aegles break his faith,
> With Ariadne, and Antiopa?
>
> (2.1.77–80)

The civilizing influence of an ordered society holds appetite in check, but it is there in the play as an alarming presence.

Peter Hyland, *An Introduction to Shakespeare: The Dramatist in His Context.* New York: St. Martin's Press, 1996, pp. 148–49.

lier, they have been reduced to sleeping "On the dank and dirty ground" (2.2.75).

Nighttime in the forest repeatedly conveys the sense of estrangement and misunderstanding with which the lovers are afflicted. When Puck creates a pitchy darkness into which he can lead Lysander and Demetrius, he is not manufacturing mischief out of nothing but is giving expression to their rivalry in love. As a stage manager of his own little play, he allows the men to parody their own tendencies toward petty vengefulness. The fact that the two young men are rather much alike, that their contention can be resolved by a simple solution (since Demetrius did in fact pay court to Helena before the play began, and need only return to his original attachment to her), adds to the sense of comedy by heightening the comic discrepancy between their anger and its lack of objective cause. Puck's manipulation serves the benign effect of showing (to the lovers themselves, in retrospect) the ridiculousness of exaggerated contentiousness. In a similar way Puck uses night and darkness as an emblem to expose the catty jealousies of the two young women and their tendency toward morbid self-pity. The effect of such cleansing exposure is a comic purgation. Puck is a creature of the night, but he uses darkness to produce ultimate illumination. He mocks pretensions, even in himself, even in the play to which he belongs: "If we shadows have offended, / Think but this, and all is mended— / That you have but slumb'red here / While these visions did appear" (5.1.412–15).

SELF-UNDERSTANDING AND DESIRE

Darkness and the forest, then, offer the lovers a glimpse of their inner selves. Often, this glimpse suggests much about human nature that is not merely perverse and jealous, but libidinous. Here again Jan Kott offers helpful insights, though he has surely gone too far. The motif on which the action of the play is based, that of escape into a forest on the eve of Mayday (Walpurgisnacht) or on Midsummer's Eve, is traditionally erotic. The four lovers are discovered the next morning asleep on the ground, in a compromising position certainly, though not in flagrante delicto. "Begin these woodbirds but to couple now?" asks Theseus humorously and continues to remain skeptical toward the lovers' story of their night—a skepticism prompted in part, one imagines, by their insistence that they have slept apart from one another. We know, in fact, that their night has been a continuous series of proposed matings without any actual consummations. "One turf shall serve as pillow for us both," Lysander suggests to Hermia as night comes on. "One heart, one bed, two bosoms, and one troth" (2.2.41–42). She finds his rhetoric pretty but insists on a propriety that is not mere primness. "Such separation as may well be said / Becomes a virtuous bachelor and a maid, / So far be distant," she instructs him (ll. 58–60). She wants her lover to move away just a little, but not too much. Hermia knows, because of the person she is, that freedom to escape the harsh Athenian law does not mean the license to try anything and that she can justify her elopement only by voluntary obedience to a code she holds to be absolutely good and that she never questions. The serpent of which she dreams, crawling on her breast to eat her heart away while Lysander watches smilingly (ll. 146–50), is not an image of her own licentiousness but of an infidelity in which she is the innocent victim. Demetrius too would never presume to take advantage of Helena's unprotected condition, however much he may perceive an opportunity for rape. . . .

Repeatedly in this play, a presumption of man's licentiousness is evoked, only to be answered by the conduct of the lovers themselves. This representation of desire almost but not quite satisfied is to be sure a titillating one, but it looks forward as do the lovers themselves to legitimate consummation in marriage and procreation. At the very end, the lovers do all go to bed while Oberon speaks of the issue that will surely spring from their virtuous coupling. Earlier, Theseus has proposed to await the marriage day for his consummation, even though he captured his wife through military force; why else should he complain of the aged moon that "lingers" his desires "Like to a stepdame or a dowager"? (Hippolyta, with a maiden's traditional reluctance, seems more content with the four-day delay than does her amorous bridegroom.) The tradesmen's play serves as one last comic barrier to the achievement of desire, although it is mercifully brief and can be performed without epilogue in the interest of further brevity. Such waiting only makes the moment of final surrender more pleasurable and meaningful.

The conflict between sexual desire and rational restraint is, then, an essential tension throughout the play reflected in the images of dark and light. This same tension exists in the nature of the fairies and of the forest. The ideal course seems to be a middle one, between the sharp Athenian law on the one hand with its threat of death or perpetual chastity, and a licentiousness on the other hand that the forest (and man's inner self) proposes with alacrity, but from which the lovers are saved chiefly by the steadfastness of the women. They, after all, remain constant; it is the men who change affections under the effect of Oberon's love potion.

COMIC REASSURANCE

This tension between licentiousness and self-mastery is closely related also to the way in which the play itself constantly flirts with genuine disaster but controls that threat through comic reassurance. Hermia is threatened with death in act 1, or with something almost worse than death—perpetual maidenhood, and yet we know already from the emphasis on love and marriage that all such threats to happiness are ultimately to prove illusory. Lysander and Hermia speak of "War, death, or sickness" and of other external threats to love, but are resolved on a plan of escape that will avoid all these. Repeatedly in the forest the lovers fear catastrophe only to discover that their senses have been deceiving them. "But who is here?" asks Helena as she comes across a sleeping man, Lysander, on the ground: "Dead, or asleep?" (2.2.100–101). When, shortly afterwards, Hermia awakes to find herself deserted, she sets off after her strangely absent lover: "Either death, or you, I'll find immediately" (l. 156). The choice seems dire, but the comic sense of discrepancy assures us that the need for such a choice is only a chimera. . . .

The fairies of *A Midsummer Night's Dream* do not govern themselves by the conventional sexual mores of the humans. As we have already seen, many things are inverted in the mirror-image world of fairydom: it is the woman rather than the man who is inconstant, the obstacles to love are internal rather than external, and so on. Similarly, the quarrel of Oberon and Titania reflects the recently completed struggle for mastery between Theseus and Hippolyta, and yet is conducted according to the peculiar customs of the fairy kingdom. Titania's love for Theseus is apparently the occasion of her current visit to Athens, in order that she may be at Theseus's wedding; yet her love for the Athenian king has taken strange forms. According to Oberon, Titania's love for Theseus prompts her to "lead him through the glimmering night / From Perigenia, whom he ravishèd, / And make him with fair Aegles break his faith, / With Ariadne, and Antiopa" (2.1.77–80). Titania to be sure denies the charge. The point is, however, that Oberon considers his queen perfectly capable of expressing her love for Theseus by encouraging him to ravish and then reject in turn a series of human mistresses. This is the sort of mysterious affection that only a god could practice or understand. Oberon's behavior in love is no less puzzling from a human vantage: he punishes Titania for denying him the changeling boy by forcing her to take a gross and foolish lover. These gods make a sport of inconstancy.

The rivalry about the changeling boy is equally bizarre if measured in human terms. Conceivably, as Kott suggests, Oberon desires the boy as his own minion, although (like so much of what Kott claims) the boy's erotic status cannot be proved from a reading of the text. We are told only that he is a "lovely boy" whom "jealous Oberon" desires as a "Knight of his train" to be his "henchman" (2.1.22–25, 121). When Oberon has succeeded in winning the boy from her, he has the youth sent to his "bower in fairyland" (4.1.60). This slender evidence seems deliberately ambiguous. Any attempts to depict Oberon as bisexual surely miss the point that the fairies' ideas concerning love are ultimately unknowable and incomprehensible. We mortals can laugh at our own libidinous tendencies when we see them mirrored in the behavior of the immortals, but we can never fathom how distant those immortals are from the ordinary pangs of human affection. Oberon is not so busy teaching Titania a lesson that he fails to enjoy Puck's "fond pageant" on the theme of human passion: "Lord, what fools these mortals be."

Titania does of course undergo an experience of misdirected love that is analogous to human inconstancy in love and that is prompted by the same love juice applied to the eyes of Demetrius and Lysander. . . . Her hours spent with Bottom are touchingly innocent and tender. Like the royal creature that she is, she forbids Bottom to leave her presence. Even if he is her slave, however, imprisoned in an animal form, she is no Circean enchantress teaching him enslavement to sensual appetite. Instead, her mission is to "purge thy mortal grossness so / That thou shalt like an airy spirit go" (3.1.145–46). It is because she is prompted by such ethereal considerations that she feeds him with apricots and dewberries, fans the moonbeams from his sleeping eyes, and the like. As Oberon reports later to Puck, having kept close watch over Titania, she graces the hairy temples of Bottom's ass's head "With coronet of fresh and fragrant flowers," (4.1.51). Rather than descending into the realm of human passion and perversity, she has attempted to raise Bottom into her own. Bottom, for his part, speaking the part of the wise fool, has noted the irrationality of love but has submitted himself to deliciously innocent pleasures that are, for him, mainly gastronomic. Titania, and Shakespeare too, have indeed purged his mortal grossness, not by making him any less funny, but by showing, how the tensions in this play between the dark and the affirmative side of love are reconciled in the image of Titania and the ass's head.

The Play's Affirmation of Patriarchy

Shirley Nelson Garner

While *A Midsummer Night's Dream* ends with a celebration of marriage and fertility, the apparently happy
ending is achieved at a high cost in its disruption of
women's mutual bonds and an affirmation of male
control over women. In the view of Shirley Nelson Garner, professor of English at the University of Min-
nesota, the play caters to the satisfaction of the psychological needs of its male characters at the expense of
the female characters. The bonds uniting Titania to her
votaress must be broken in Oberon's scheme, and the
play seems to assert that the bonds of friendship between Hermia and Helena must be severed in order to
make them ready for marriage. According to Garner,
the total silence of Hermia and Helena in the play's last
act serves to affirm their newfound subservience and
the triumph of patriarchy in the play.

> Jack shall have Jill;
> Nought shall go ill;
> The man shall have his mare again,
> and all shall be well.
>
> (III.ii.461–64, Signet Classic)

More than any of Shakespeare's comedies, *A Midsummer
Night's Dream* resembles a fertility rite, for the sterile world that
Titania depicts at the beginning of Act II is transformed and the
play concludes with high celebration, ritual blessing, and the
promise of regeneration. Though this pattern is easily apparent
and has often been observed, the social and sexual implications
of the return of the green world have gone unnoticed. What has
not been so clearly seen is that the renewal at the end of the
play affirms partiarchal order and hierarchy, insisting that the
power of women must be circumscribed, and that it recognizes
the tenuousness of heterosexuality as well. The movement of

the play toward ordering the fairy, human, and natural worlds is also a movement toward satisfying men's psychological needs, as Shakespeare perceived them, but its cost is the disruption of women's bonds with each other.

Regeneration finally depends on the amity between Titania and Oberon. As she tells him, their quarrel over possession of an Indian boy has brought chaos, disease, and sterility to the natural world:

And this same progeny of evils comes
From our debate, from our dissension;
We are their parents and original.

(II.i.115–17)

The story of the "lovely boy" is told from two points of view, Puck's and Titania's. Puck tells a companion fairy that Oberon is "passing fell and wrath" because Titania has taken as her attendant "a lovely boy, stolen from an Indian king"; he continues:

She never had so sweet a changeling.
And jealous Oberon would have the child
Knight of his train, to trace the forest wild.
But she perforce withholds the lovèd boy,
Crowns him with flowers, and makes him all her joy.
And now they never meet in grove or green,
By fountain clear, or spangled starlight sheen,
But they do square, that all the elves for fear
Creep into acorn cups and hide them there.

(II.i.18–31)

Shortly afterward, when Oberon tells Titania that it is up to her to amend their quarrel and that he merely begs "a little changeling boy" to be his "henchman," she retorts, "Set your heart at rest./ The fairy land buys not the child of me." Then she explains the child's origin, arguing her loyalty to the child's mother to be the reason for keeping him:

His mother was a vot'ress of my order,
And, in the spicèd Indian air, by night,
Full often hath she gossiped by my side,
And sat with me on Neptune's yellow sands,
Marking th' embarkèd traders on the flood;
When we have laughed to see the sails conceive
And grow big-bellied with the wanton wind;
Which she, with pretty and with swimming gait
Following—her womb then rich with my young squire—
Would imitate, and sail upon the land,
To fetch me trifles, and return again,
As from a voyage, rich with merchandise.
But she, being mortal, of that boy did die;

And for her sake do I rear up her boy,
And for her sake I will not part with him.

(II.i.121–37)

Both accounts affirm that the child has become the object of Titania's love, but the shift in emphasis from one point of view to the other is significant. . . .

OBERON'S VICTORY, TITANIA'S LOSS

Oberon's winning the boy from Titania is at the center of the play, for his victory is the price of amity between them, which in turn restores the green world. At the beginning, Oberon and Titania would seem to have equal magical powers, but Oberon's power proves the greater. Since he cannot persuade Titania to turn over the boy to him, he humiliates her and torments her until she does so. He uses the love potion not simply to divert her attention from the child, so that he can have him, but to punish her as well. As he squeezes the love flower on Titania's eyes, he speaks a charm—or rather a curse—revealing his intention:

> What thou see'st when thou dost wake,
> Do it for thy truelove take;
> Love and languish for his sake.
> Be it ounce, or cat, or bear,
> Pard, or boar with bristled hair,
> In thy eye that shall appear
> When thou wak'st, it is they dear.
> Wake when some vile thing is near.

(II.ii.27–34)

When Puck tells him that Titania is "with a monster in love" (III.ii.6), he is obviously pleased: "This falls out better than I could devise" (1.35).

Though the scenes between Titania and Bottom are charming and hilarious, Titania is made ridiculous. Whereas her opening speech is remarkable for its lyric beauty, and her defense of keeping the Indian boy has quiet and dignified emotion power, now she is reduced to admiring Bottom's truisms and his monstrous shape: "Thou art as wise as thou art beautiful" (III.i.147). However enjoyable the scenes between her and Bottom, however thematically satisfying in their representation of the marriage of our animal and spiritual natures, Titania, free of the influence of Oberon's love potion, says of Bottom, "O, how mine eyes do loathe his visage now!" (V.i.80). By his own account, Oberon taunts Titania into obedience. . . .

Oberon gains the exclusive love of Titania and also possession of the boy to whom he is attracted. But his gain is Titania's loss: she is separated from the boy and, in that separation, further severed from the woman whom she had loved. Oberon can offer ritual blessings at the play's end because he has what he wanted from the beginning: Titania obedient and under his control and the beautiful Indian boy in his bower.

LIMITING WOMEN'S POWER

Like the fairy king, the two men in power in the human world, Theseus and Egeus, want to attain the exclusive love of a woman and, also, to accommodate their homoerotic desires. In order to do so, they, like Oberon, attempt to limit women's power, and their success or failure to do so affects their participation in the cosmic world.

The opening of *A Midsummer Night's Dream* puts Hippolyta's subjugation in bold relief as Theseus reminds his bride-to-be:

> Hippolyta, I wooed thee with my sword,
> And won thy love, doing thee injuries;
> But I will wed thee in another key,
> With pomp, with triumph, and with reveling.

(I.i.16–19)

Capturing Hippolyta when he defeated the Amazons, Theseus has abducted her from her Amazon sisters to bring her to Athens and marry her. Though most directors play Hippolyta as a willing bride, I once saw San Francisco's Actors' Workshop, following the cues of Ian Kott, bring her on stage clothed in skins and imprisoned in a cage. The text invites such a rendering, for almost immediately it sets her apart from Theseus by implying that she sides with Hermia and Lysander against Egeus and Theseus, when he sanctions Egeus's authority. After Theseus tells Hermia to prepare to marry Demetrius or "on Diana's altar to protest/For aye austerity and single life" (I.i.89–90) and then beckons Hippolyta to follow him offstage, he undoubtedly notices her frowning, for he asks, "What cheer, my love?" (I.i.122). Shakespeare heightens her isolation by presenting her without any Amazon attendants.

Though Theseus is less severe than Egeus, he is, from the outset, unsympathetic toward women. The first words he speaks, voicing the play's first lines and first image, must be taken as a sign: the moon "lingers" his desires, he tells Hippolyta, "Like a stepdame, or a dowager,/Long withering out

a young man's revenue." He utterly supports Egeus as patri-
arch, telling Hermia:

> To you your father should be as a god,
> One that composed your beauties; yea, and one
> To whom you are but as a form in wax
> By him imprinted and within his power
> To leave the figure or disfigure it.
>
> (I.i.47–51)

As a ruler, he will enforce the law, which gives Egeus control over Hermia's sexuality and embodies patriarchal order.
Though he has heard that Demetrius has won Helena's
heart but now scorns her, and has meant to speak to him
about it, "My mind did lose it" (I.i.114). A lover-and-leaver of
women himself, he undoubtedly identifies with Demetrius
and forgets his duty toward Helena. He exits inviting Egeus
and Demetrius to follow and talk confidentially with him,
suggesting his spiritual kinship with them. . . .

THE BREAKING OF BONDS

Whereas the separation of Hippolyta and Titania from other
women is implied or kept in the background, the breaking of
women's bonds is central in the plot involving the four young
lovers. Demetrius and Lysander are divided at the outset, but
the play dramatizes the division of Hermia and Helena. Fur-
thermore, their quarreling is more demeaning than the men's.
And once Demetrius and Lysander are no longer in competi-
tion for the same woman, their enmity is gone. Hermia and Helena, on the contrary, seem permanently separated and apparently give over their power to the men they will marry. Once
their friendship is undermined and their power diminished,
they are presumably "ready" for marriage.

Hermia's fond recollection of her long-standing and inti-
mate friendship with Helena calls attention to Helena's dis-
loyalty, occasioned by the latter's desire to win Demetrius's
thanks and to be near him. Telling her friend that she intends to run away with Lysander, Hermia recalls:

> And in the wood, where often you and I
> Upon faint primrose beds were wont to lie,
> Emptying our bosoms of their counsel sweet,
> There my Lysander and myself shall meet.
>
> (I.i.214–217)

Just as Helena breaks her faith with Hermia to ingratiate
herself with Demetrius, so later she will believe that Hermia

has joined with men against her. Deeply hurt, Helena chastizes Hermia:

> Is all the counsel that we two have shared,
> The sister's vows, the hours that we have spent,
> When we have chid the hasty-footed time
> For parting us—O, is all forgot?
> All school days friendship, childhood innocence?
> We, Hermia, like two artificial gods,
> Have with our needles created both one flower,
> Both on one sampler, sitting on one cushion,
> Both warbling of one song, both in one key;
> As if our hands, our sides, voices, and minds,
> Had been incorporate. So we grew together,
> Like to a double cherry, seeming parted,
> But yet an union in partition,
> Two lovely berries molded on one stem;
> So, with two seeming bodies, but one heart;
> Two of the first, like coats in heraldry,
> Due but to one, and crownèd with one crest.
> And will you rent our ancient love asunder,
> To join with men in scorning your poor friend?
> It is not friendly, 'tis, not maidenly.
> Our sex, as well as I, may chide you for it,
> Though I alone do feel the injury.

(III.ii.198–219)

In a scene that parallels in its central position Titania's wooing of Bottom, the rupture of their friendship becomes final. They accuse and insult each other, with Hermia calling Helena a "juggler," "canker blossom," "thief of love," "painted maypole"; and Helena naming her a "counterfeit" and a "puppet" (III.ii.282–296). Their quarrel becomes absurd as it turns on Hermia's obsession, taken up by both Lysander and Helena, that Lysander has come to prefer Helena because she is taller. Though no other women characters in Shakespeare's plays come close to fighting physically, Hermia threatens to scratch out Helena's eyes (III.ii.297–98). Her threat is serious enough to make Helena flee. Lysander is made equally ridiculous in his abrupt change of heart; yet he and Demetrius are spared the indignity of a demeaning quarrel and leave the stage to settle their disagreement in a "manly" fashion, with swords. Even though Puck makes a mockery of their combat through his teasing, they are not so thoroughly diminished as Hermia and Helena.

In the course of the play, both Hermia and Helena suffer at the hands of their lovers. Betrothed to Helena, Demetrius deserts her for Hermia. When she pursues him, he tells her that she makes him sick (II.i.212) and threatens to rape her (II.214–219). By doggedly following him, she maintains a kind of desperate power over him. She will not play Dido to his Aeneas. Consequently, he cannot sustain the image of the romantic rake, whose women pine and die, commit suicide, or burn themselves on pyres when he leaves them. Disappointed in his love for Hermia, he cannot get loose from Helena. Yet her masochism undercuts her power:

> I am your spaniel; and, Demetrius,
> The more you beat me, I will fawn on you.
> Use me but as your spaniel, spurn me, strike me,
> Neglect me, lose me; only give me leave,
> Unworthy as I am, to follow you.
> What worser place can I beg in your love—
> And yet a place of high respect with me—
> Than to be usèd as you use your dog?
>
> (II.1.202–210)

When Helena is in a position of positive power with both Lysander and Demetrius in love with her, she cannot take advantage of it because she assumes that she is the butt of a joke. And of course, in a sense, she is right: she is the victim of either Puck's prank or his mistake. Hermia must also bear Lysander's contempt. In the forest, he insists that he "hates" her (III.ii.270, 281) and calls her outrageous names: "cat," "burr," "vile thing," "tawny Tartar," "loathèd med'cine," "hated potion," "dwarf," "minimus, of hind'ring knotgrass made," "bead," "acorn" (III.260–64, 328–330). While both women protest their lovers' treatment of them, neither can play Beatrice to her Benedick. Both more or less bear their lovers' abuses.

After the four lovers sleep and awaken coupled as they will marry, Hermia and Helena do not reconcile. Once they leave the forest, they lose their voices. Neither of them speaks again. Recognizing that it is difficult for an actor to be on stage without any lines, as Helena and Hermia are for almost all of Act V, Shakespeare was undoubtedly aware that he was creating a portentous silence. Since Helena and Hermia are evidently married between Acts IV and V, their silence suggests that in their new roles as wives they will be obedient, allowing their husbands dominance.

THE COST OF HARMONY

The end of *A Midsummer Night's Dream* is as fully joyous as the conclusion of any of Shakespeare's comedies. No longer

angry with each other, Oberon and Titania bring blessing to
the human world:

> Hand in hand, with fairy grace,
> Will we sing, and bless this place.

(V.i.398–99)

Though Oberon calls up dark possibilities, he offers a charm
against them. The prospect of love, peace, safety, and prosperity is as promising as it ever will be. The cost of this harmony, however, is the restoration of patriarchal hierarchy,
so threatened at the beginning of the play. This return to the
old order depends on the breaking of women's bonds with
each other and the submission of women, which the play relentlessly exacts. Puck's verse provides the paradigm:

> Jack shall have Jill;
> Nought shall go ill;
> The man shall have his mare again,
> and all shall be well.

If we turn to some of Shakespeare's comedies in which
women's bonds with each other are unbroken and their
power is left intact or even dominates, the tone of the ending
is less harmonious or even discordant. In *The Merchant of
Venice,* for example, where Portia is in control and she and
Nerissa triumph over Gratiano and Bassanio, there is no ritual celebration. Portia directs the scene and carefully cir-
cumscribes her marriage with Bassanio to close out Anto-
nio. When she and Nerissa reveal their identities as the
doctor and the clerk, they make clear their extraordinary
power to outwit and deceive, calling up women's ultimate
destructive power in marriage and love—to cuckold. The
final moments of the play move toward reconciliation, but
not celebration. The last line, a bawdy joke, is spoken by
Gratiano, the most hatefilled character in the play, and reminds us of men's fear of women and their need to control
them: "While I live I'll fear no other thing/So sore, as keeping safe Nerissa's ring" (V.i.306–307).

In *Love's Labor's Lost,* where the women remain together
and in control, there is no comic ending. Echoing Puck,
Berowne makes the point as he speaks to the King of
Navarre:

> Our wooing doth not end like an old play;
> Jack hath not Jill. These ladies' courtesy
> Might well have made our sport a comedy.

When the King replies, "Come, sir, it wants a twelvemonth

and a day,/And then 'twill end," Berowne answers, "That's too long for a play" (V.ii.872–76). The refrains of the closing songs call forth images of cuckolding and of "greasy Joan" stirring the pot.

The pattern of these comic endings suggests that heterosexual bonding is tenuous at best. In order to be secure, to enjoy, to love—to participate in the celebration that comedy invites—men need to maintain their ties with other men and to sever women's bonds with each other. The implication is that men fear that if women join with each other, they will not need men, will possibly exclude them or prefer the friendship and love of women. This is precisely the threat of the beautiful scene that Titania describes between herself and her votaress. This fear may be based partially on reality, but it is also partially caused by projection: since men have traditionally had stronger bonds with other men than with women and have excluded women from participation in things about which they cared most, they may assume that women, granted the opportunity, will do the same. Given this possibility or likelihood, Shakespeare's male characters act out of a fear of women's bonding with each other and a feeling of sexual powerlessness. The male characters think they can keep their women only if they divide and conquer them. Only then will Jack have Jill; only then will their world flourish.

Reason and Imagination in the Final Act

Michael Mangan

According to British scholar Michael Mangan, some readers of the play assume that Theseus "stands as spokesman for the values which the play endorses" in the last act of *A Midsummer Night's Dream*. In this view, rational pragmatism triumphs over irrational imagination, which is apparently only useful for amending poor dramatic performances if Theseus is to be believed. In the following essay, Mangan contests this view, arguing that Theseus stands for an aesthetic of power, and that his judgement of the imagination is ironically undercut throughout the fifth act. It is undercut not only by what the audience has observed on stage, but also by Hippolyta's defense of the lovers' dream, and most importantly, by the presence of the fairies after the humans have gone to bed.

It is sometimes assumed that Theseus, in the final act at least, stands as spokesman for the values which the play endorses. Such an assumption contributes to those readings of the play which condemn it for 'pandering to an aristocratic ideology' (Freedman). But is this really the case?

Certainly, in the final act of the play, Theseus puts forward a model of stage-audience relationships which seems on first sight to be unexceptionable. Asked to choose his wedding-night entertainment, he rejects a scholarly satire on learning, the eunuch's song about the battle of the centaurs, and a version of *The Bacchae*. . . . Theseus, against the advice of his Master of the Revels, opts for the local am-dram group, performing 'A tedious brief scene of young Pyramus and his love Thisbe: very tragical mirth'.

THESEUS I will hear that play
    For never anything can be amiss
    When simpleness and duty tender it.
    Go bring them in; and take your places, ladies.
HIPPOLYTA I love not to see wretchedness o'ercharged,
    And duty in his service perishing.
THESEUS Why gentle sweet, you shall see no such thing.
HIPPOLYTA He says they can do nothing in this kind.
THESEUS The kinder we, to give them thanks for nothing.
    Our sport shall be, to take what they mistake,
    And what poor duty cannot do
    Noble respect takes it in might, not merit.

                                        (V, i, ll. 81–92)

What Theseus has to say here sounds very much like a text-book account of the Elizabethan stage. It echoes the ideas of theatre expressed in the Prologue to *Henry V*, which insist that dramatic meaning is created through a dynamic and creative interplay between stage and audience. . . .

As he goes on to elaborate his dramatic theory, however, Theseus rather spoils the effect:

Where I have come, great clerks have purposèd
To greet me with premeditated welcomes,
Where I have seen them shiver and look pale,
Make periods in the midst of sentences,
Throttle their practised accent in their fears,
And in conclusion dumbly have broke off,
Not paying me a welcome. Trust me, sweet,
Out of this silence yet I picked a welcome,
And in the modesty of fearful duty
I read as much as from the rattling tongue
Of saucy and audacious eloquence.

                                        (V, i, ll. 93–103)

If Theseus's initial remarks about the drama seem well-intentioned, his choice of illustration sounds a more sinister note. The analogy of the inept performer and the civic functionary, terrified to the point of speechlessness before the warrior lord, might not be as reassuring to the Amazon Queen as he might have expected. By reminiscing at this point about the terror he inspires in others, making even 'great clerks . . . shiver and look pale', Theseus emphasizes the power of life or death which he holds in actuality over those who speak in his company. We may remember Hermia at the start of the play, facing the possibility of a death sentence; or the mechanicals' nervousness at the prospect of misjudging their performance and being too frightening. Even Theseus' new bride was gained by conquest in battle, as he himself had earlier reminded her: 'I wooed thee with my sword, And won thy love doing thee injuries' (I, i. ll. 16–17).

THESEUS AND RATIONAL CONTROL

Theseus's aesthetic is an aesthetic of power. Although apparently resembling the Prologue in *Henry V*, it differs from it in emphasis. Listening to the clerks, Theseus 'hears' the welcome which they are too frightened to speak; listening to the play, he intends to 'take what they mistake'. In both cases Theseus remains in control: *he* decides what meanings he wants to hear.

And if we suspect that Theseus's judgment of the things of the imagination might not, after all, be perfect, we have only to look at the speech with which he began the scene, the famous statement of his world-view. Here he speaks as a rational, no-nonsense pragmatist, the sort of man for whom dreams and fairytales are nothing more than make-believe:

> HIPPOLYTA 'Tis strange, my Theseus, that these lovers
>   speak of.
> THESEUS More strange than true. I never may believe
>   These antique fables, nor these fairy toys.
>   Lovers and madmen have such seething brains,
>   Such shaping fantasies, that apprehend
>   More than cool reason ever comprehends.
>   The lunatic, the lover and the poet
>   Are of imagination all compact:
>   One sees more devils than vast hell can hold;
>   That is the madman: the lover, all as frantic,
>   Sees Helen's beauty in a brow of Egypt:
>   The poet's eye, in a fine frenzy rolling,
>   Doth glance from heaven to earth, from earth to
>   to heaven;
>   And as imagination bodies forth
>   The forms of things unknown, the poet's pen
>   Turns them to shapes and gives to airy nothing
>   A local habitation and a name.
>   Such tricks hath strong imagination,
>   That if it would but apprehend some joy,
>   It comprehends some bringer of that joy:
>   Or, in the night, imagining some fear,
>   How easy is a bush supposed a bear!
>
>   (V, i, ll. 1–22)

Theseus' speech links 'lovers and madmen', performing in a phrase what the middle of the play itself enacts in its setting and structure. But he links them only to dismiss them both. Theseus sees his task as being to rationalize. His analysis upholds the values of 'cool reason' over those of 'shaping fantasies', and his confident eloquence seems at first to prevail. Hippolyta, however, is unconvinced:

> HIPPOLYTA But all the story of the night told over
> And all their minds transfigured so together
> More witnesseth than fancy's images,
> And grows to something of great constancy.
>
> (V, i, ll. 23–6)

And in all sorts of ways, even as he speaks, Theseus's position is undercut. Firstly, of course, there is the basic joke that Theseus, himself the creation of a 'poet's pen', is here denying the very creative act that gave him breath to speak. That irony is compounded by the fact that the character whom Shakespeare chooses to represent Athenian logic is not Plato, Socrates or Aristotle—not, that is, one of the philosophers of ancient history—but Theseus, a creature himself of myth and legend. The ironic undercutting of his speech, moreover, is clear enough, for we, the audience, *know* that he is wrong. We have seen Acts II, III and IV of the play, and we know that whatever account the lovers gave of it, the 'truth' is more outlandish than Theseus's well-ordered world can conceive of. In Theseus's limited world-view there is room only for the truth of everyday, common-sense experience: all that lies beyond that is 'antique fable', and that which is 'strange' is almost certainly not also 'true'. We know better.

Theseus's aesthetic is not to be taken seriously. He hardly takes it very serious himself. When the performance of 'Pyramus and Thisbe' starts the actors are accorded none of the 'noble respect' which he talks about to Hippolyta; Theseus and his courtiers continually attempt to take over the performance, repeatedly heckling and interrupting the action with their witticisms and criticisms.

> THESEUS This fellow does not stand upon points.
> LYSANDER He hath rid his prologue like a rough colt: he
> knows not the stop . . .
> THESEUS I wonder if the lion be to speak.
> DEMETRIUS No wonder, my lord, when walls are so wilful
> to hear without warning . . .
> LYSANDER This lion is a very fox for his valour.
> THESEUS True, and a goose for his discretion.
> DEMETRIUS Not so, my lord, for his valour cannot carry his
> discretion, and the fox carries the goose.
> THESEUS His discretion, I am sure, cannot carry his valour,
> for the goose carries not the fox.
>
> (V, i, ll. 117–9, 151–3, 205–8, 228–33)

These are typical of the aristocrats' interruptions. What the actors mistake, they take and turn into their own form of entertainment. They take over the meanings of the story and read them in their own ways. '"Merry" *and* "tragical"?' Theseus had earlier asked, '. . . How shall we find the concord of this discord?' (V, i, ll. 58, 60). In fact they do not find concord at all, since the play that the mechanicals stage and the one which the aristocrats witness are two different things. Hippolyta puts it succinctly in answer to Theseus.

> THESEUS The best in this kind are but shadows, and the
>   worst are no worse if imagination amend them.
> HIPPOLYTA It must be your imagination, then, and not theirs.
>   (V, i. ll. 212–14)

The mechanicals present a touching tragedy; Duke Theseus and his friends watch a pure farce.

TWO DIFFERENT AUDIENCES

And so do we, of course. We are implicated in the process as well. If the aristocrats sneer at the incompetence of Bottom and his friends, the real-life audience is also invited to feel superior to these bumbling amateurs, and to laugh at their naïve attempts at play-making. Perhaps we would laugh at them even more if it were not for the continual interruptions of Theseus, Demetrius and Lysander. The on-stage audience and the real-world audience ought, in theory, to be in agreement here; they should be similarly 'placed' in relation to the action of the mechanicals' play. But by one of those seesaw effects which is endemic to the theatre, the more the aristocrats sneer at the 'common folk', the less we may want to align ourselves with them. The witty, sophisticated jests of the privileged at the expense of the artisan classes wear thin rather quickly, with the result that the real-world audience is confronted with two alternative possible responses, neither of which is completely satisfactory in itself. Simply to laugh at the mechanicals and to align oneself with the sneering courtiers and their ungenerous reactions is uncomfortable; yet the invitation to join in with that laughter is unmistakably there.

And perhaps this is the point: that Theseus once more is wrong. Wrong because the mechanicals' play somehow survives the superior jibings of the wedding party. The mechanicals have conquered their qualms about misjudging the tone of the piece, and present their play with some con-

fidence. The irrepressible Nick Bottom gives the performance of his life, and dances the bergomask at the end. Even
Robin Starveling, playing the part of Moon, battles on
through the audience's chattering to deliver his lines. The
real-world audience are offered a glimpse of something beyond the surface of the bad performance: the Pyramus and
Thisbe story is a burlesque, of course, of *Romeo and Juliet*,
but it is also a comment on the stories of the lovers in the
Dream itself, some of whom were also initially separated by
parental jealousy. The lovers, if only they could see it, are
watching what might have happened to them: 'Pyramus and
Thisbe' is a reminder of the tragic potentials within the story
which we have seen turn out happily. Perhaps a glimmer of
this does eventually get through to the cynical on-stage audience of aristocrats. As Bottom/Pyramus bewails the supposed death of Flute/Thisbe, Hippolyta says 'Beshrew my
heart, but I pity the man' (V, i. ll. 285)—and it is even possible that she is not being ironic here.

Such a reading of Hippolyta's line would be consistent
with the mood of *A Midsummer Night's Dream* as a whole: it
would resonate with the sense which permeates the play
that meanings above and beyond those of Theseus's rational
world can be glimpsed at unexpected moments. Bottom's
'dream' speech typifies this.

> BOTTOM . . . I have had a most rare vision. I have had a dream
> past the wit of man to say what dream it was. Man is but an
> ass if he go about t'expound this dream. Methought I was—
> there is no man can tell what. Methought I was, and
> methought I had—but man is but a patched fool if he will of-
> fer to say what methought I had. The eye of man hath not
> heard, the ear of man hath not seen, man's hand is not able
> to taste, his tongue to conceive, nor his heart to report what
> my dream was. I will get Peter Quince to write a ballad of
> this dream. It shall be called 'Bottom's Dream', because it
> hath no bottom, and I will sing it in the latter end of a play,
> before the Duke.
>
> (IV, i, ll. 198–214)

The memory is there, yet Bottom's language cannot quite
deal with it. Time and again words fail him, and the language of the senses collapses into nonsense ('The eye of man
hath not heard . . .'). But this is not just a jibe at an under-
educated artisan. As meaning slips away from him, Bottom
backs away from his attempts to articulate his experience.
We can never describe our dreams quite as they were when

we experienced them; as Freud acknowledged, 'we distort dreams in attempting to reproduce them'. Bottom holds out some hope that art may succeed where 'ordinary' language fails, but Peter Quince's ballad never gets written, or at least it is never performed before the Duke. (It may be, of course, that this is the redundant Epilogue which Theseus turns down in favour of the bergomask dance.) Yet in another sense, Bottom's Dream *has* been written down, and we have watched it being staged. Again, we are faced with two apparent opposites: that the dream is unrepresentable, and that we have seen it represented.

A SERIES OF FALSE ENDINGS

What of the very end of the play? As the story draws to a close the fairies take over the stage space once more, unknown to the mortals. Their presence is ambiguous: haunting the palace they are a reminder of the wilder subconscious energies that lie hidden beneath the civilized surface. They are also there to bless the marriages, and in this, finally, surely we see that celebration of aristocratic ideology?

> To the best bride bed will we
> Which by us shall blessèd be,
> And the issue there create
> Ever shall be fortunate . . .
> And the blots of nature's hand
> Shall not in their issue stand.
> Never mole, harelip, nor scar,
> Nor mark prodigious such as are
> Despisèd in nativity
> Shall upon their children be.
>
> (V, ii, ll. 33–6, 39–44)

The gesture is there, certainly: the fairies, who in English folklore are so rarely benevolent towards human children, bestow their blessings on the offspring of these particular unions. What is striking, though, is how this is contextualized. The blessing of the couples is almost lost in a series of dramatic flourishes in which, in its last few minutes, *A Midsummer Night's Dream* plays games with the conventions of dramatic closure.

The play finishes with a series of false endings; several times it teases the audience with the possibility of an ending, only to come back to life again. The process actually started at the end of Act IV, where the lovers' story seemed all but over. Their statement about returning to the court could have signalled the end of the action (as it does in *As You Like It*), but Bottom, who has slept through their discovery, suddenly wakes up and lets us know that there is more to come. Then, once 'Pyramus and Thisbe' has been performed *A Midsummer Night's Dream* appears about to finish too: 'Will it please you to see the Epilogue, or to hear a Bergomask dance between two of our company?' (V, v, ll. 346–8) asks Bottom. Theseus chooses the bergomask and the play is ended by a dance—a common practice in the Elizabethan playhouse, of course. But the dance ends and the play continues. Theseus steps forward and delivers a speech which clears the stage of all the actors:

> The iron tongue of midnight hath told twelve.
> Lovers, to bed; 'tis almost fairy time . . .
>   Sweet friends, to bed.
> A fortnight hold we this solemnity
> In nightly revels and new jollity.

(V, i, ll. 349–50, 354–6)

The audience is getting ready to clap by now—but the clearing of the stage is not quite complete: as the mortal characters make their exit, Puck steps forward to deliver an epilogue.

> Now the hungry lion roars,
> And the wolf behowls the moon . . .
> And we fairies, that do run
> By the triple Hecate's team
> From the presence of the sun,
> Following darkness like a dream,
> Now are frolic; not a mouse
> Shall disturb this hallowed house.
> I am sent with broom before
> To sweep the dust behind the door.

(V, i, ll. 373–4, 385–92)

This should be an even more definite cue for the action to end, as Puck's last couplet begins to question his own status: is he supernatural being or actor-cum-stage-hand? The Epilogue's traditional task of modulating from the world of the fiction back to the world of the audience's everyday reality seems to have been accomplished. But again the ending is a false one. Oberon and Titania return to the stage for their final number. A speech, then a song and dance. Once more the play seems to have ended—but no, Oberon has yet to bless the marriage beds before the stage empties again. Surely, this must be the end? No, once again, Puck frustrates the potential moment of closure. He stays—or returns—for one final address to the audience, modulating more completely now into the actor who asks for applause rather than the 'serpent's tongue' of the audience's hisses. Even in this speech Shakespeare cannot resist one last twitch of the rope: 'So goodnight unto you all', says Puck, but stays yet another moment for his punchline:

> Give me your hands if we be friends
> And Robin shall restore amends.

(Epilogue, l. 16)

Now, finally, the play really is over. Like Nick Bottom's Pyramus, it has staved off its own death several times, but finally it relaxes its grip on the spectators and allows them to applaud if they will, and then to leave the theatre, to go back to their homes, their lives. This series of false endings, the continual uncertainty as to whether the play is actually over yet, has placed the audience in a position at the end of the play which is rather like that of the lovers at the end of Act IV, Scene ii—unsure which world they inhabit, that of fantasy or of reality, but faced with the claims of both. It is another rebuttal of Theseus's 'cool reason'.

CHRONOLOGY

1509

Publication of *The Praise of Folly* by the Christian humanist Erasmus. Henry VIII becomes king of England.

1516

Sir Thomas More's *Utopia* published.

1517

Martin Luther posts his 95 Theses, sparking the Reformation movement.

1535

Sir Thomas More beheaded for treason by Henry VIII.

1536

The Protestant leader John Calvin completes his influential *Institutes of the Christian Religion.* Death of Erasmus.

1542

English translation of the French romance *Huon of Bordeaux,* an influence on *A Midsummer Night's Dream*, is published.

1543

Publication of Copernicus's *On the Revolution of Celestial Spheres,* which contended that the earth was not the center of the universe.

1545–63

The Council of Trent, start of the Catholic Counter-Reformation.

1558

Queen Elizabeth becomes queen of England; rules until 1603. Marguerite de Navarre, *Heptameron.*

1561

Publication of English translation of Castiglione's *The Courtier.*

1564

Birth of William Shakespeare at Stratford-upon-Avon. Birth of Christopher Marlowe at Canterbury. Deaths of John Calvin and Michelangelo.

1567

Publication of Golding's translation of Ovid's *Metamorphoses,* a major influence on Shakespeare.

1569

Shakespeare's father, John, elected bailiff (or mayor) of Stratford.

1572

Birth of Ben Jonson, Shakespeare's play-writing rival and friend. Birth of the poet John Donne.

1576

First public playhouse, the Theatre, opens in London.

1579

Publication of the English translation of Plutarch's *Lives of the Noble Grecians and Romans,* an influence on *A Midsummer Night's Dream.*

1580

Michel de Montaigne, *Essays.*

1582

Marriage of William Shakespeare and Anne Hathaway.

1583

Birth of the Shakespeare's first child Susanna.

1585

Birth of the Shakespeare's twins, Judith and Hamnet.

1586

Death of Sir Philip Sidney, the most admired Elizabethan courtier and "Renaissance man."

1588

Defeat of the Spanish Armada, the attempted invasion of England.

c. 1590

Christopher Marlowe writes his hit play *Doctor Faustus.*

c. 1590–93

Shakespeare's earliest plays are written and publicly performed, including *Titus Andronicus, The Comedy of Errors,* and *Richard III.*

1592

The Rose Theater is built in London. Plague closes London playhouses for two years. Shakespeare publicly attacked as an "upstart" playwright; a public apology follows.

1593

Christopher Marlowe killed in a tavern brawl.

1594

Shakespeare, *Romeo and Juliet.* Shakespeare's troupe of players is designated the Lord Chamberlain's Men. First record of Lord Chamberlain's Men performing for Queen Elizabeth.

1595

Shakespeare, *A Midsummer Night's Dream.*

1597

Shakespeare, *Henry IV, Part 1*; Sir Francis Bacon, *Essays.* Shakespeare buys New Place, probably the largest house in Stratford at the time.

1599

The Globe Theater built in London; Shakespeare is a major shareholder. Death of Edmund Spenser, England's most noted poet. Shakespeare, *Henry V, As You Like It, Julius Caesar.*

c. 1600

Shakespeare, *Hamlet.*

1603

Queen Elizabeth dies; accession of James I as king of England. Shakespeare's Company becomes known as the King's Men, and they begin performing frequently in the royal court.

1603–1606

Shakespeare writes some of his greatest tragedies: *Othello, Macbeth,* and *King Lear.*

1604

Shakespeare, *Measure for Measure.*

1605

Cervantes, *Don Quixote*; Bacon, *The Advancement of Learning.*

1607

Jamestown Colony (named after King James) is established in Virginia.

1610

Galileo announces his telescopic discoveries.

1611

The King James translation of the Bible is published. Shakespeare, *The Tempest.*

1613

The Globe Theater burns down; rebuilt the next year.

1616

Death of William Shakespeare at age 52.

1620

Pilgrims settle at Plymouth, Massachusetts.

1623

Publication of Shakespeare's collected plays in a Folio edition. Death of Anne Hathaway Shakespeare.

1633

Posthumous publication of the poetry of John Donne (d. 1631).

1642

English theaters closed down by the Puritans; not re-opened until 1660.

1667

Publication of John Milton's epic poem *Paradise Lost.*

For Further Research

SHAKESPEARE'S LIFE AND TIMES

Richard Dutton, *William Shakespeare: A Literary Life*. New York: St. Martin's, 1989.

Philip Edwards, *Shakespeare: A Writer's Progress*. New York: Oxford University Press, 1986.

Russell Fraser, *Young Shakespeare*. New York: Columbia University Press, 1988.

Roland M. Frye, *Shakespeare's Life and Times: A Pictorial Record*. Princeton, NJ: Princeton University Press, 1967.

Park Honan, *Shakespeare: A Life*. Oxford: Oxford University Press, 1998.

Peter Hyland, *An Introduction to Shakespeare: The Dramatist in His Context*. New York: St. Martin's, 1996.

David Scott Kastan, ed., *A Companion to Shakespeare*. Oxford: Blackwell Publishers, 1999.

Dennis Kay, *Shakespeare: His Life and Times*. New York: Twayne, 1995.

Francois Laroque, *The Age of Shakespeare*. New York: Harry N. Abrams, 1993.

Peter Levi, *The Life and Times of William Shakespeare*. New York: Henry Holt, 1989.

A.L. Rowse, *William Shakespeare: A Biography*. New York: Harper & Row, 1963.

Samuel Schoenbaum, *Shakespeare: His Life, His Language, His Theater*. New York: Penguin, 1990.

——, *William Shakespeare: A Compact Documentary Life*. Oxford: Oxford University Press, 1987.

SHAKESPEAREAN THEATER

G.E. Bentley, *The Profession of Player in Shakespeare's Time 1590–1642*. Princeton, NJ: Princeton University Press, 1984.

M.C. Bradbrook, *The Rise of the Common Player*. Cambridge, MA: Harvard University Press, 1962.

Alan C. Dessen, *Elizabethan Stage Conventions and Modern Interpreters.* Cambridge, England: Cambridge University Press, 1984.

Andrew Gurr, *Playgoing in Shakespeare's London.* 2nd ed. Cambridge, England: Cambridge University Press, 1996.

———, *The Shakespearean Stage.* 3rd ed. Cambridge, England: Cambridge University Press, 1992.

Michael Hattaway, *Elizabethan Popular Theatre.* London: Routledge, 1987.

Thomas Marc Parrott and Robert Hamilton Ball, *A Short View of Elizabethan Drama.* New York: Charles Scribner's Sons, 1943.

Meredith Anne Skura, *Shakespeare the Actor and the Purposes of Playing.* Chicago: University of Chicago Press, 1993.

EDITIONS OF *A MIDSUMMER NIGHT'S DREAM*

Harold F. Brooks, ed., *A Midsummer Night's Dream.* London and New York: Methuen, 1979.

John Russell Brown, ed., *A Midsummer Night's Dream.* New York and London: Applause Books, 1996.

R.A. Foakes, ed., *A Midsummer Night's Dream.* Cambridge, England: Cambridge University Press, 1984.

Peter Holland, ed., *A Midsummer Night's Dream.* Oxford: Clarendon Press, 1994.

Barbara A. Mowat and Paul Werstine, eds., *A Midsummer Night's Dream.* New York: Washington Square, 1993.

Gail Kern Paster and Skiles Howard, eds., A Midsummer Night's Dream: *Texts and Contexts.* Boston: Bedford/St. Martin's, 1999.

THE PLAY IN PERFORMANCE

John Russell Brown, *Shakespeare's Plays in Performance.* New York: Applause Books, 1993.

Jay L. Halio, *A Midsummer Night's Dream.* Manchester and New York: Manchester University Press, 1994.

Robert Hapgood, "Shakespeare on Film and Television," in *The Cambridge Companion to Shakespeare Studies.* Ed. Stanley Wells. Cambridge, England: Cambridge University Press, 1986.

Roger Warren, A Midsummer Night's Dream: *Text and Performance.* London: Macmillan, 1983.

Gary Jay Williams, *Our Moonlight Revels:* A Midsummer Night's Dream *in the Theatre.* Iowa City: University of Iowa Press, 1997.

STUDIES OF *A MIDSUMMER NIGHT'S DREAM*

C.L. Barber, "May Games and Metamophoses on a Midsummer Night," in *Shakespeare's Festive Comedy*. Princeton, NJ: Princeton University Press, 1959.

Harold Bloom, ed., *William Shakespeare's* A Midsummer Night's Dream. New York and Philadelphia: Chelsea House, 1987.

John Russell Brown, "Love's Truth and the Judgements of *A Midsummer Night's Dream* and *Much Ado About Nothing*," in *Shakespeare and His Comedies*. London: Methuen, 1957.

James L. Calderwood, *A Midsummer Night's Dream*. New York: Twayne, 1992.

William C. Carroll, "*A Midsummer Night's Dream*: Monsters and Marriage," in *The Metamorphoses of Shakespearean Comedy*. Princeton, NJ: Princeton University Press, 1985.

R.W. Dent, "Imagination in *A Midsummer Night's Dream*," *Shakespeare Quarterly* 15 (1964):115–29.

Richard Dutton, ed., *A Midsummer Night's Dream*. London: Macmillan Press, 1996.

Stephen Fender, *Shakespeare:* A Midsummer Night's Dream. London: Edward Arnold, 1968.

Harley Granville-Barker, "Preface to *A Midsummer Night's Dream*," in *More Prefaces to Shakespeare*. Ed. Edward M. Moore. Princeton, NJ: Princeton University Press, 1974.

Germaine Greer, "Love and the Law," in *Politics, Power, and Shakespeare*. Ed. Frances McNeely Leonard. Arlington: Texas Humanities Research Center, 1981.

Helen Hackett, *A Midsummer Night's Dream*. Plymouth, UK: Northcote House, 1997.

Jonathan Gil Harris, "Puck/Robin Goodfellow," in *Fools and Jesters in Literature, Art, and History*. Ed. Vicki K. Janik. Westport, CT and London: Greenwood Press, 1998.

R. Chris Hassel Jr., "'Most Rare Vision': Faith in *A Midsummer Night's Dream*," in *Faith and Folly in Shakespeare's Romantic Comedies*. Athens: University of Georgia Press, 1980.

Peter Hollindale, *A Midsummer Night's Dream*. London: Penguin Books, 1992.

J. Dennis Huston, "Parody and Play in *A Midsummer Night's Dream*," in *Shakespeare's Comedies of Play*. New York: Columbia University Press, 1981.

Dorothea Kehler, ed., *A Midsummer Night's Dream: Critical Essays*. New York and London: Garland Publishing, 1998.

Jan Kott, "Titania and the Ass's Head," in *Shakespeare Our Contemporary*. Trans. Boleslaw Taborski. London: Routledge, 1988.

Alexander Leggatt, *"A Midsummer Night's Dream,"* in *Shakespeare's Comedy of Love*. London: Methuen, 1974.

Michael Mangan, *"A Midsummer Night's Dream,"* in *A Preface to Shakespeare's Comedies: 1594–1603*. London: Longman, 1996.

Philip C. McGuire, "Hippolyta's Silence and the Poet's Pen," in *Speechless Dialect: Shakespeare's Open Silences*. Berkeley: University of California Press, 1985.

Ronald F. Miller, *"A Midsummer Night's Dream*: The Fairies, Bottom, and the Mystery of Things," *Shakespeare Quarterly* 26 (1975):254–68.

Louis A. Montrose, *"A Midsummer Night's Dream* and the Shaping Fantasies of Elizabethan Culture: Gender, Power, Form," in *Rewriting the Renaissance: the Discourses of Sexual Difference in Early Modern Europe*. Eds. Margaret W. Ferguson, Maureen Quilligan, and Nancy J. Vickers. Chicago and London: University of Chicago Press, 1986.

Ruth Nevo, "Fancy's Images," in *Comic Transformations in Shakespeare*. London: Methuen, 1980.

Paul H. Olson, *"A Midsummer Night's Dream* and the Meaning of Court Marriage," *ELH: English Literary History* 24 (1957):95–119.

Anthony W. Price, ed., *Shakespeare,* A Midsummer Night's Dream: *A Casebook*. London: Macmillan, 1983.

David P. Young, *Something of Great Constancy: The Art of* A Midsummer Night's Dream. New Haven, CT: Yale University Press, 1966.

INDEX